COACHING HIGH PERFORMANCE SOCCER

By Giovanni Trapattoni

REEDSWAIN SOCCER VIDEOS & BOOKS

and

Edizioni Nuova Prhomos

REEDSWAIN INC
612 Pughtown Road
Spring City, Pensylvania 19475
1-800-331-5191
www,REEDSWAIN.COM
ISBN No.1-890946-37
Library of Congress Catalog Number 00-101755

May 1999

3, via O. Bettacchini
06012 Città di Castello (Pg), ITALY
tel. +390758550805, fax. +390758521167
Cover photo by Foto Sabe
Translated by Sestilio Polimanti

Printed by Grafiche Tevere

Index

One quarter of a century and... the papers with my early notes yellow with age. From soccer and its magic....to soccer as a show-business, permanent technical-tactical evolution and continuously updated conditioning.
Mass-media, sponsors, business, pay-per-view tv, globalization, the acceleration of the technological era, the internet, etc.... and the difficulty in keeping the memory of one's own roots.

Introduction

It is not easy to discuss the tactical evolution of high performance soccer. Such a discussion is subject to misunderstandings and the tone could become academic. This is why I am not going to provide a detailed explanation of every "historical change", with references to national teams, clubs or players. Instead, in order to give clarity and consistency to the following chapters I will make use of what the "HISTORY" of soccer has provided, that is the changes that have taken place over the years in this now global sport.
In particular, I would like to point out that all that is contained in this book is based on personal concepts and experiences deriving from professional soccer.
Chapter 1 contains a synthesis of the main "historical changes"; that is, the most striking changes put into practice by players, and their description, through sequences, with the help of diagrams to better explain their technical-tactical content.
Chapter 2 deals with a very important subject for the soccer of the third millennium: the player and his "role", no longer linked to objective standards as it was in the soccer of the 1960s and 1970s, but built on a constant improvement both in the attacking and in the defensive phase.
The physical conditioning at the beginning of the soccer season is dealt with in Chapter 3, along with the annual physical, technical and tactical planning for a high performance team (Bayern Munich), considering all the matches of the season (both official and friendly/scrimmages).
My point of view on matters related to the psychological-physical conditioning of the players are also found in this book.

Giovanni Trapattoni

Symbols

ball

movement of the ball – direct pass

spin pass

movement with the ball

movement of the player

movement of the player from a starting position

player

player with the ball

opponent

direction of play

coach

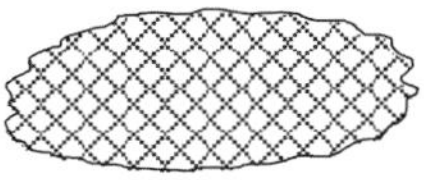

free space

orientation of the player

Chapter 1

TACTICAL EVOLUTION IN HIGH PERFORMANCE SOCCER AND RELATED COACHING METHODS

- Introduction
- Phase of possession of the ball
- Phase of non-possession of the ball

Introduction

Soccer is said to have started in 1863 in England and for a certain period it mantained uniform systems of play and related uniform tactics.
The earliest evolutions took place after the introduction of new rules, for example, the one about off-side players. This determined the change from the "**pyramidal**" (the method at the beginning of the 1900s) to the **W-M-shaped** arrangement in 1925.
Some coaches, Karl Rappan for instance, introduced the Rigel system (or "catenaccio", literally "bolt" from the idea of blocking the opposing attack), while South America preferred a 4-2-4 arrangement, perfected into a 4-3-3 by Brazil's national team at the 1958 World Cup in Sweden.
From that moment on, every national team developed their own schemes and arrangements, sometimes drawn from those of the clubs of their country.
In 1962 England turned the original Brazilian 4-2-4 into a 4-1-3-2; in 1970 Brazil showed a flexible 4-4-2 arrangement, which Germany also used in 1974.
Thanks to the achievements of Inter Milan, AC Milan and the Italian national team between 1960 and 1980, Italy became one of the most heterogeneous countries from the point of view of schemes: ***il calcio all'italiana*** (soccer the Italian way) provided for a player placed behind the defense line, the sweeper.
At the beginning of the 70s, Ajax and the Dutch national team made a remarkable contribution to the technical-tactical evolution of soccer: the tactics of pressure, off-side and double-teaming (or double-marking) can all be ascribed to them. Dutch soccer also introduced versatility, total soccer, the importance of team play and players that did not identify with the "old" role any more (backs became wing players).
This revolution was not accepted by everybody: in fact, in the 1974 World Cup in Germany many national teams were arranged with a man-marking defense, using players in specific roles.
In the 1978 World Cup in Argentina, many national teams were ready to apply the Dutch innovations: Argentina, Brazil and Sweden showed an overall tactical improvement, with a defense arranged along the same line and schemes developed from the Dutch ones.
From that moment on, the search for developing and improving every tactical constituent began: the number of versatile players increased. The so-called "role" player would not be identified as such any more. "Man-marking play" gradually turned to zone or mixed-zone play. Every club or

national team developed arrangements and schemes derived from zone arrangement: among them, Belgium with the 4-3-3 and France with the 4-4-2 (winner of the 1984 European Cup) were the national teams to have evolved the most around the technical-tactical principles connected with zone-play[1].

From those years on, new rules (for example, the ones about goalkeeping, the possibility of expelling the player fouling the opponent when the former is the last man before the goal, the possibility of being called in for a tactical foul), the players' increased skills in kicking the ball from set plays near the penalty area, the three points for wins and the greater speed of play, have deeply modified the technical-tactical principles, thus also changing coaching methods.

---

[1] We should not forget Lobanowsky's Russia and their 3-5-2.

PHASE OF POSSESSION OF THE BALL

Paragraph A - Searching for, creating and occupying space in the midfield.

Paragraph B - Occupying space in the attack on the right wing.

B_1 Occupying space in depth on the right wing.

B_2 Occupying space at the edge of the penalty area.

B_{3a} Occupying space in the attack - Cutting in.

B_{3b} Penetration of a midfielder into a central position - zone.

B_{3c} Penetration of a midfielder onto a wing.

Paragraph C - Creating space in depth.

Paragraph D - Building up the play on the wings - Search for superiority in numbers.

Paragraph E - Educational coaching.

PHASE OF NON-POSSESSION OF THE BALL

Paragraph F - Double-teaming.
Tactical dialogue - Verbal communication.

Paragraph G - Pressure – Counterpressure.
Educational and coaching exercises.

Paragraph H - The off-side tactics.

PHASE OF POSSESSION OF THE BALL

I will now analyze those technical-tactical matters which I have had to deal with in my experience as a coach.
In 1990, in my introduction to Emilio Cecchini's book "Il processo della formazione tattica" I wrote: "....besides, pressure applied by more players on the man with the ball along with the occupation of nearby spaces, double-teaming and highly effective defensive systems have reduced the available spaces, thus creating new problems for players and coaches: the evolution of today's soccer depends also on their solution....".
I had guessed right. In fact, the tactical adaptations required to solve these problems have also had to consider another fundamental factor in today's soccer: quick play and high pace throughout the match.
Considering the basic concepts of soccer (shown in table 1)

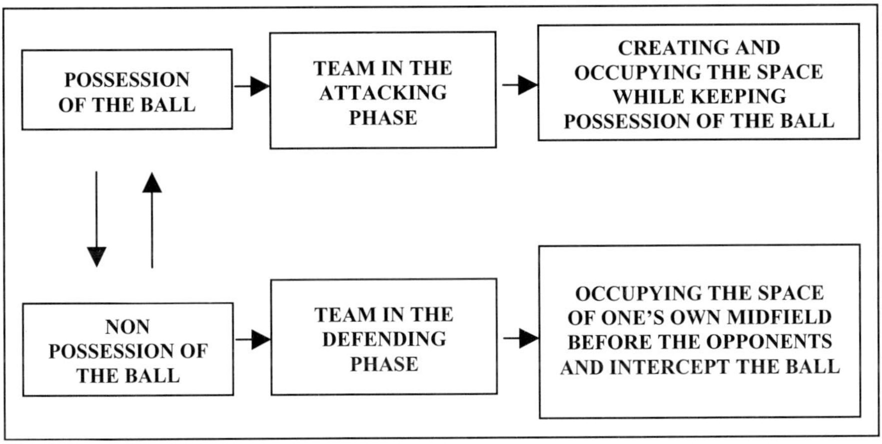

Table 1 - Basic concepts of soccer.

and the arrangement and the organization of the zone or mixed-zone play teams (usually short and tight, see diagrams 1 and 2), the main problem I had to solve when my players were **in possession of the ball** was the one of creating space: searching for, creating and occupying space in the different parts of the field, and exploiting that space in an effective and positive way.
In the following schemes, the opposing team is arranged according to zone or mixed-zone play: every diagram (the soccer field or parts of it with the

positioned players) represents the **method**, and can be used as a reference for developing the action according to the set objective.
The opponent's presence is always considered "active" for **coaching purposes**. Such a presence does not manifest itself with all the "possible" options, but only with the "feasible" ones.

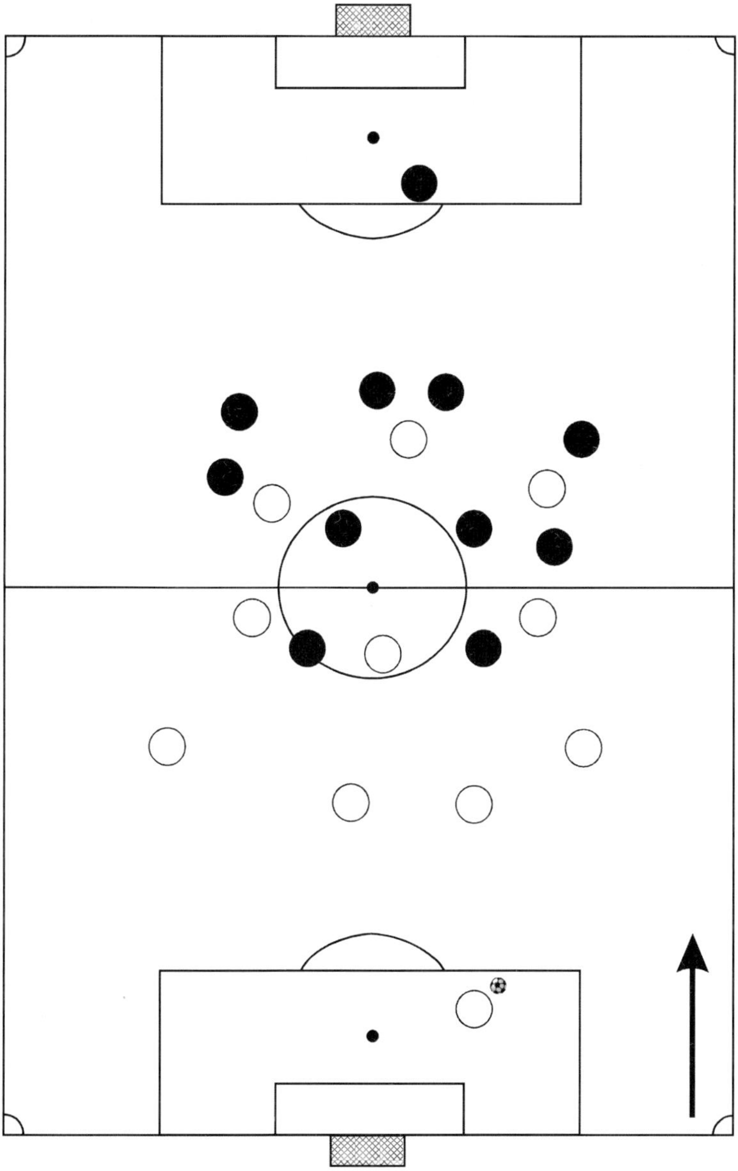

○ - **Team arranged according to the 4-3-3**

● - **Team arranged according to the 4-4-2**

Diagram 1 - "Short and tight" teams when the goalkeeper returns the ball.
N.B.: For coaching purposes only.

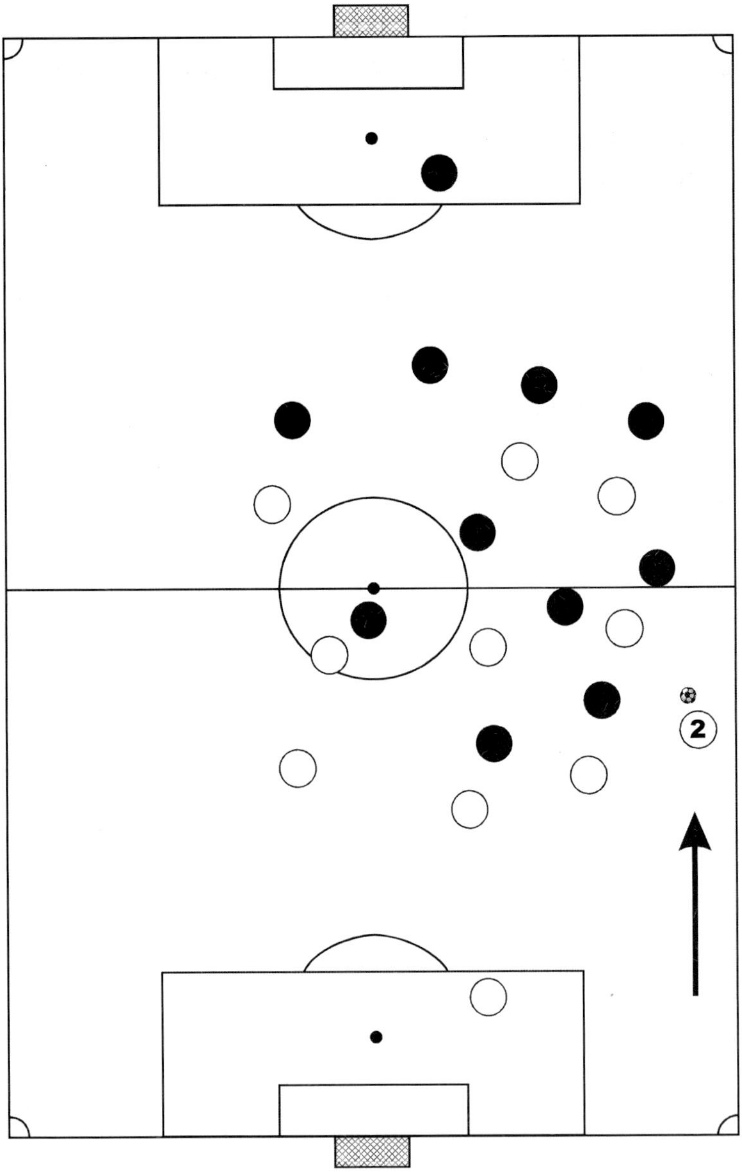

Diagram 2 - "Short and tight" teams with player 2 in possession of the ball.
N.B.: For coaching purposes only.

Paragraph A

Searching for, Creating, and Occupying Space in the Midfield

First phase of play:

- **Conditions**: the team being coached is arranged according to the 4-3-3 and is in possession of the ball. The opposing team is arranged according to the 4-4-2.
- **Phases of play**: player 4 dribbles the ball and passes it towards the free space.
  Player 7 moves to receive the ball.
  Player D has two options:

1. He can remain in the space he occupied before the pass from player 4 (diagram 3).

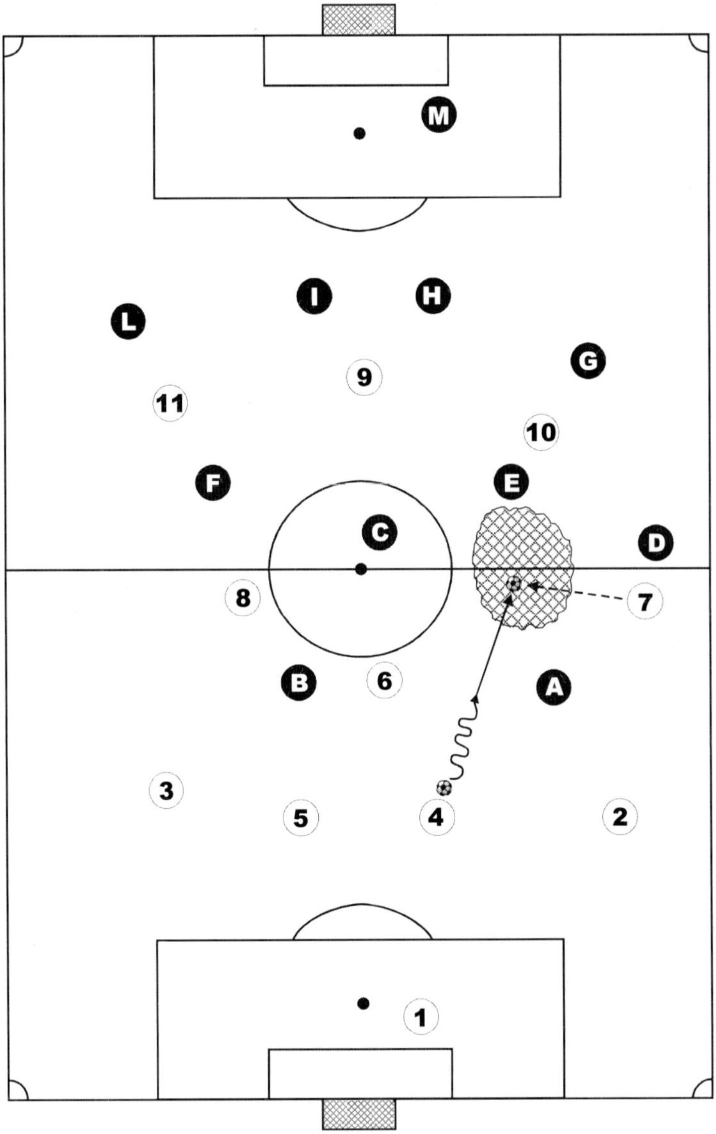

Diagram 3

2. He can follow the movement of player 7 and mark him. If he chooses this option, a free space will be created on the midfield right wing for the penetration of player 2 (diagram 4).

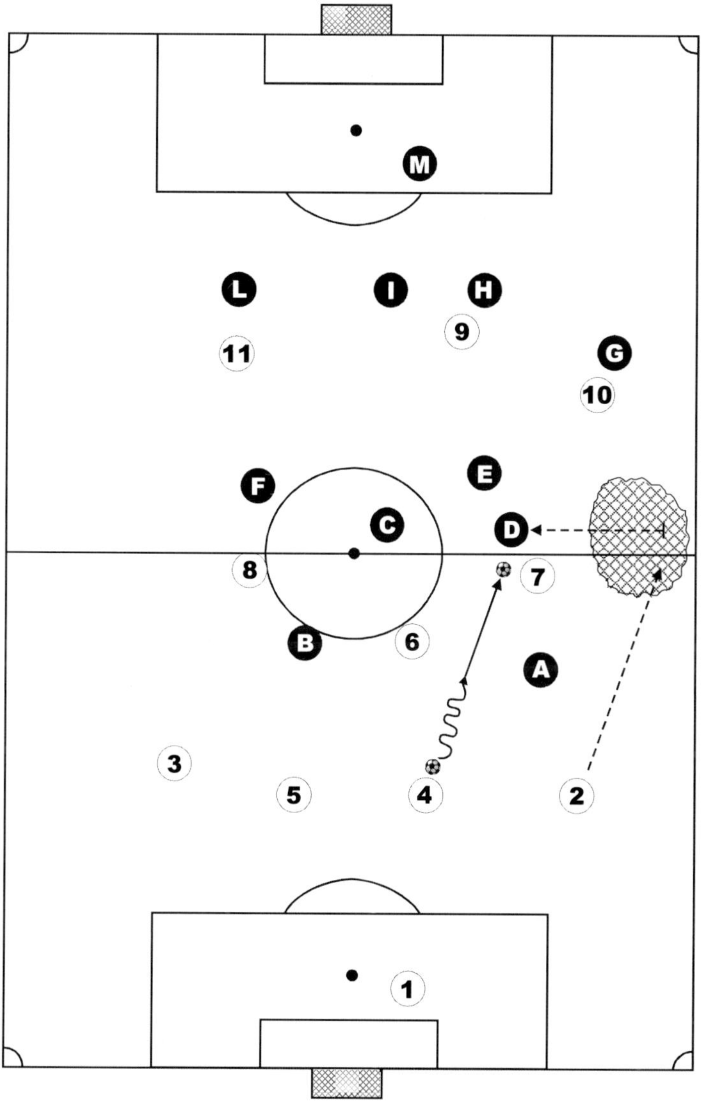

Diagram 4

Paragraph B
Occupying Space in the Attack on the Right Wing

Second phase of play:

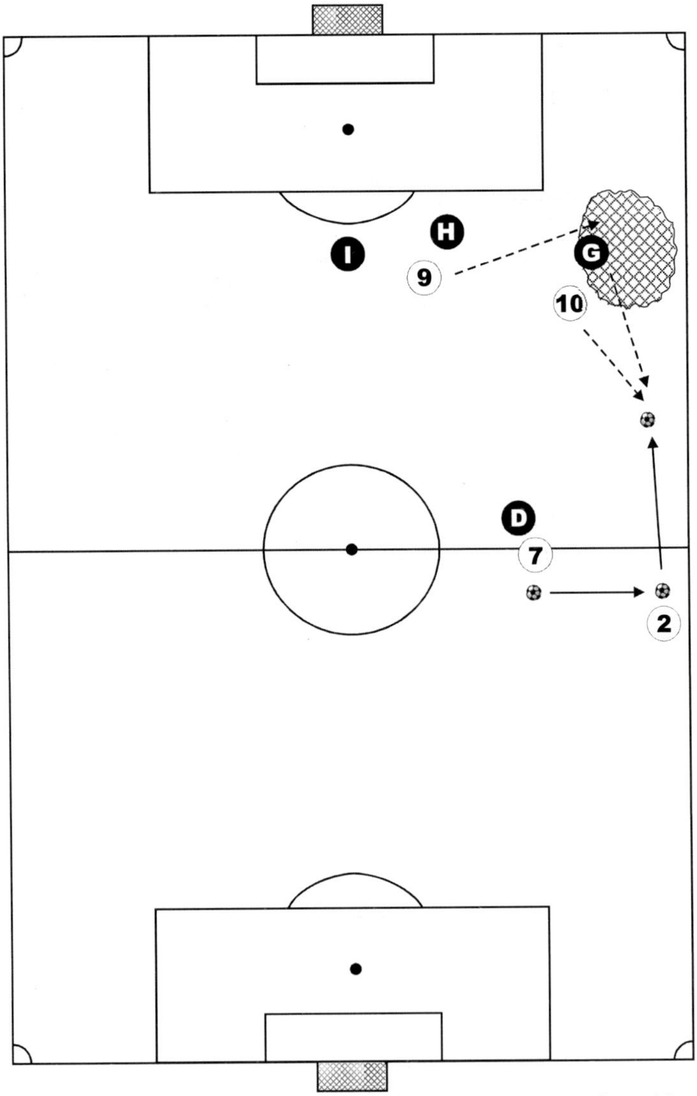

Diagram 5 - Player 7 passes the ball to player 2; player 2 passes it to 10 who, running towards the ball followed by opponent G (placing pressure on the man with the ball) creates space for the penetration of player 9 onto the wing.

Paragraph B_1
Occupying Space in Depth on the Right Wing

Second phase of play - First option:

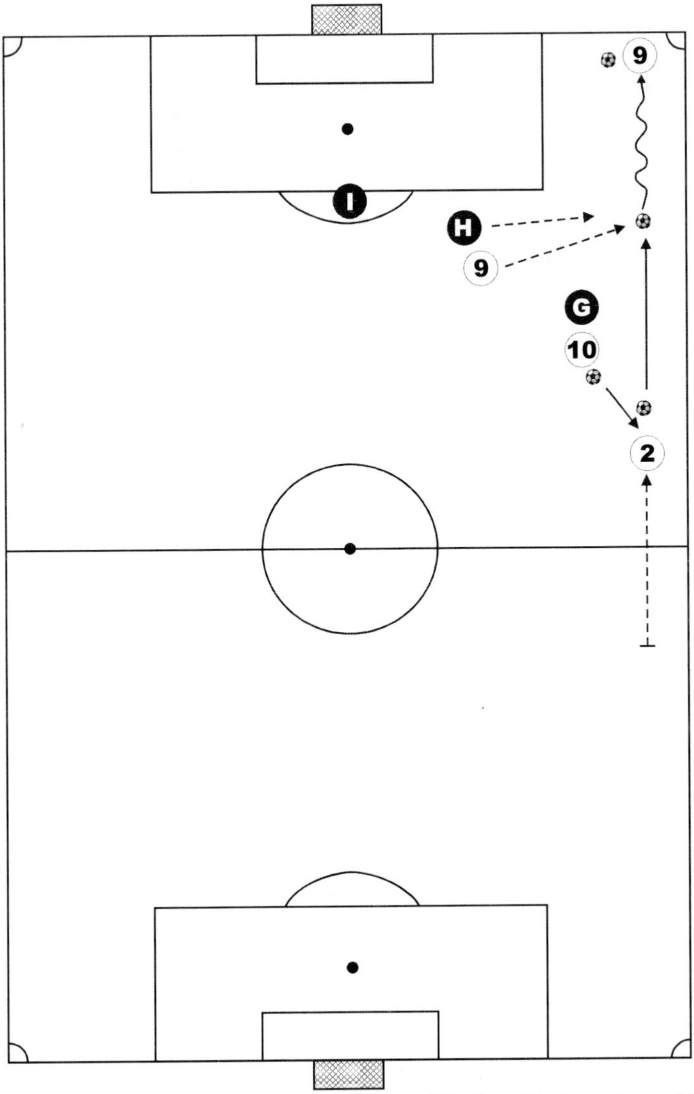

Diagram 6 - Player 2 receives a back pass from 10. Considering player 9's penetration, player 2 can make a deep pass to player 9 who has an advantage over opposing H and therefore a chance to make a cross pass from the end of the field.

Paragraph B_2

Occupying Space at the Edge of the Penalty Area

Second phase of play - Second option:

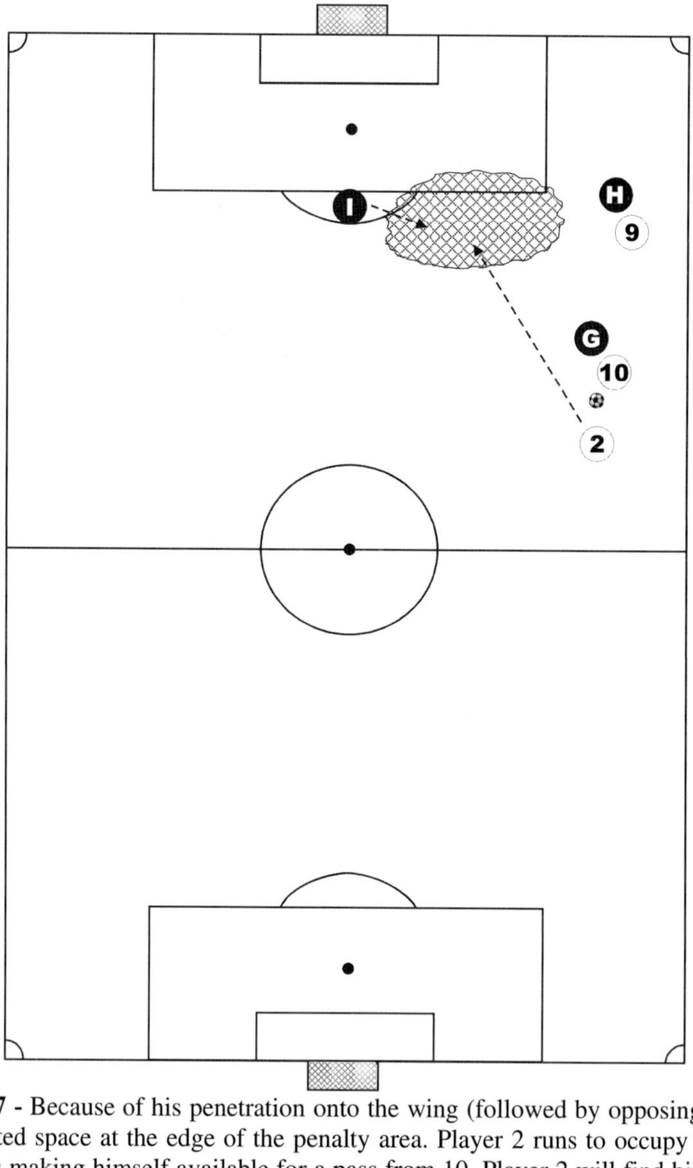

Diagram 7 - Because of his penetration onto the wing (followed by opposing H), player 9 has created space at the edge of the penalty area. Player 2 runs to occupy the vacated space, thus making himself available for a pass from 10. Player 2 will find himself in a 1 on 1 situation with his opponent, facing the goal and with high chance of scoring.

Paragraph B_3
Occupying Space in the Attack - Cutting in

Third phase of play - First opportunity - Second option:

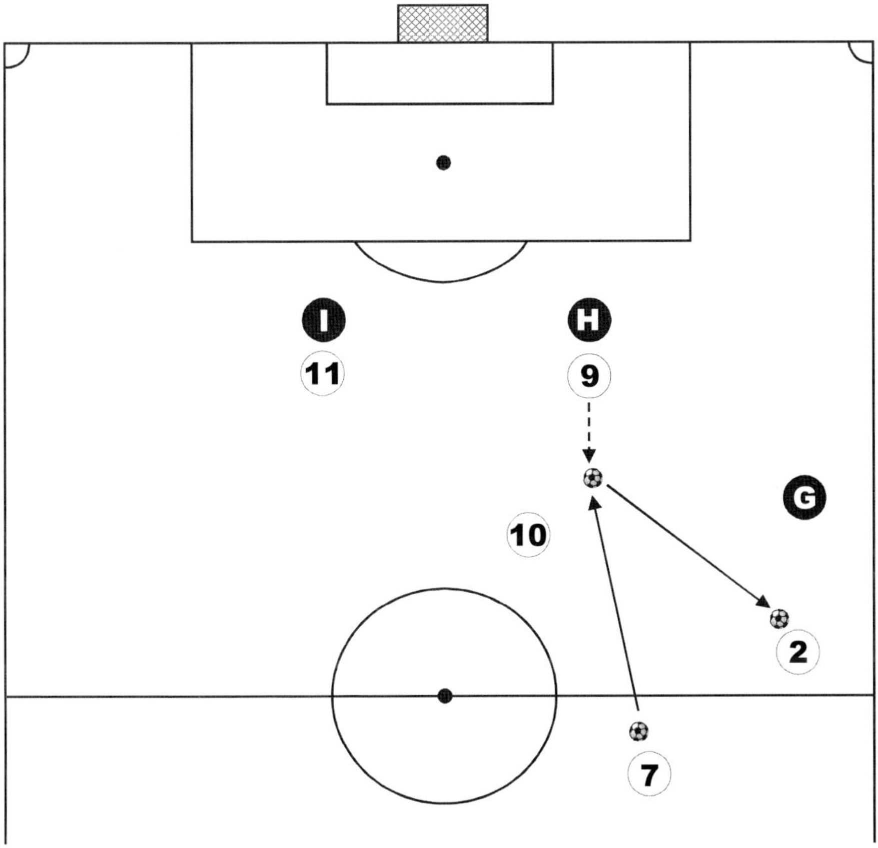

Diagram 7a - Player 9 runs to the ball to receive the pass from 7, then passes it to 2.

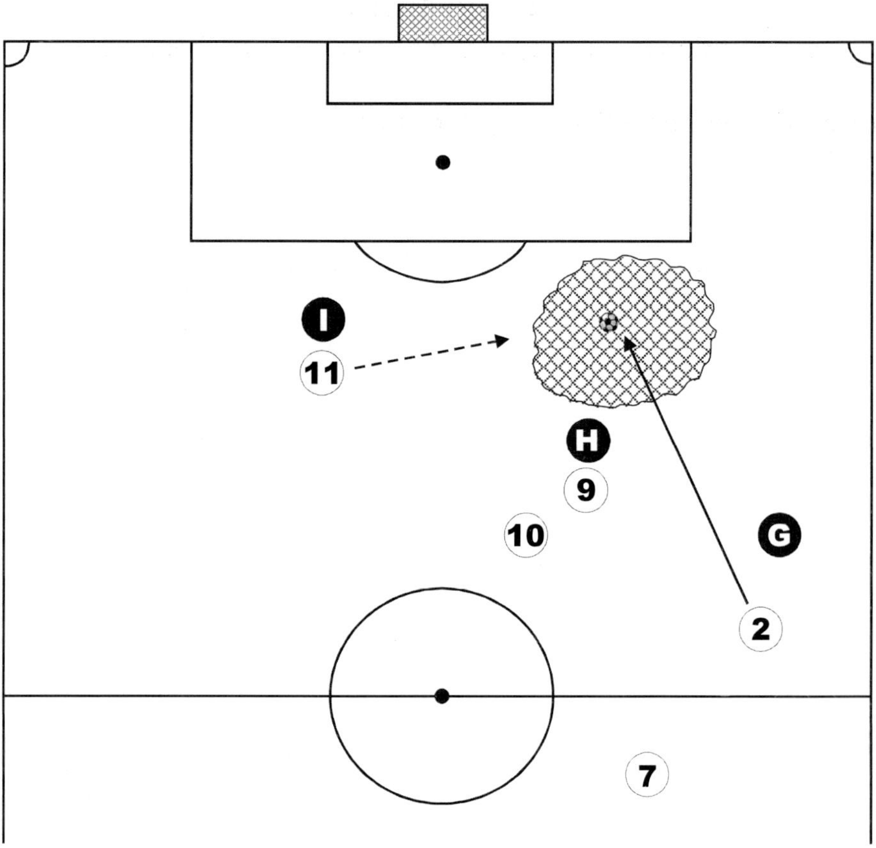

Diagram 7b - Followed by opposing player H, player 9 creates space at his back where 2 can pass the ball to 11 who cuts in.

Paragraph B_{3a}

Penetration of a Midfielder into a Central Position - Zone

Third phase of play - Second opportunity:

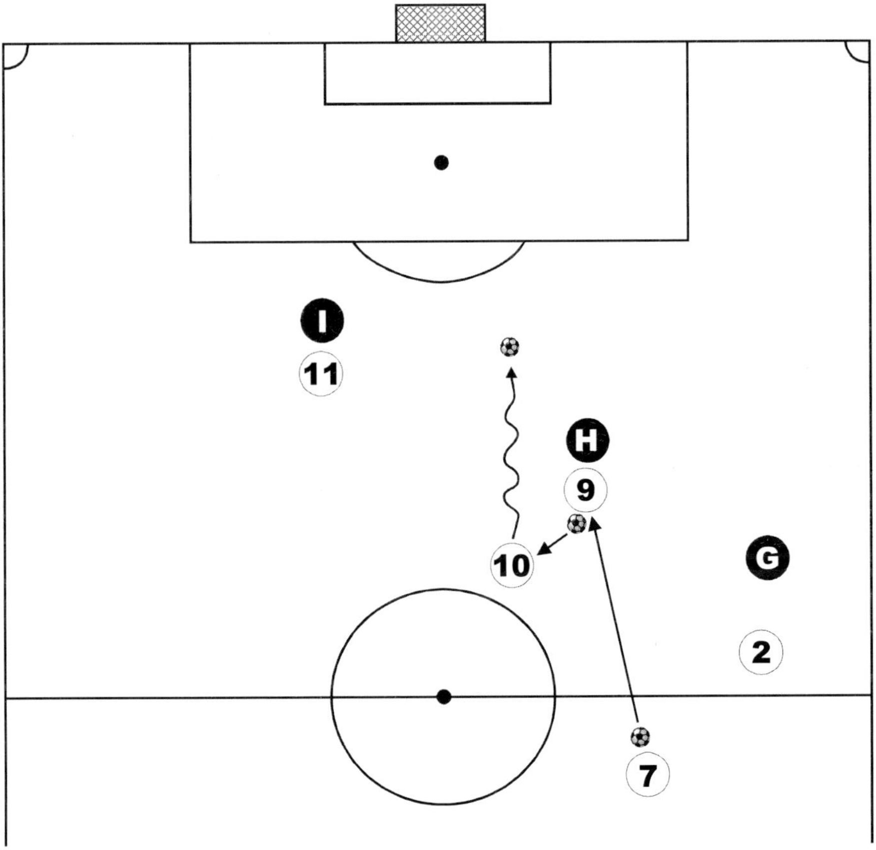

Diagram 7c - Player 9 is pressured by player H. When he receives the ball from 7, instead of making a pass to player 2 he passes the ball to midfielder 10, thus creating an opportunity for 10's penetration.

Paragraph B_{3b}

Penetration of a Midfielder onto a Wing

Third phase of play - Third opportunity:

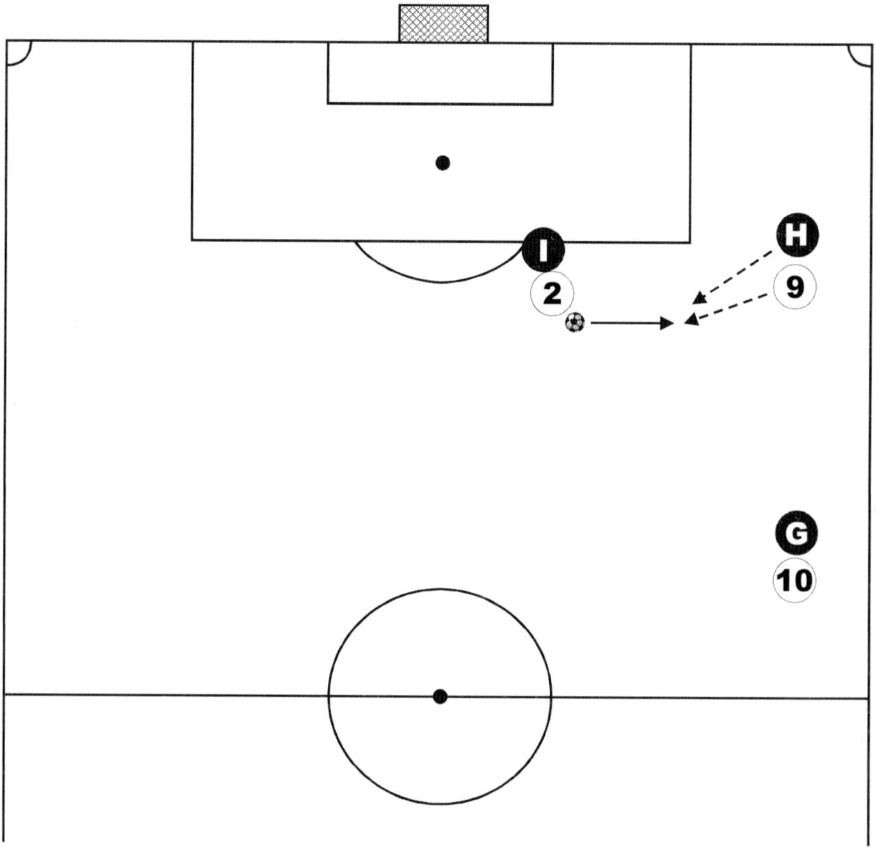

Diagram 8 - If player 2 cannot dribble past opponent I, he places himself with his "back to the opponent" - thus acting as a "reference" - and asks player 9 for cooperation: 9 runs towards him and receives the pass.

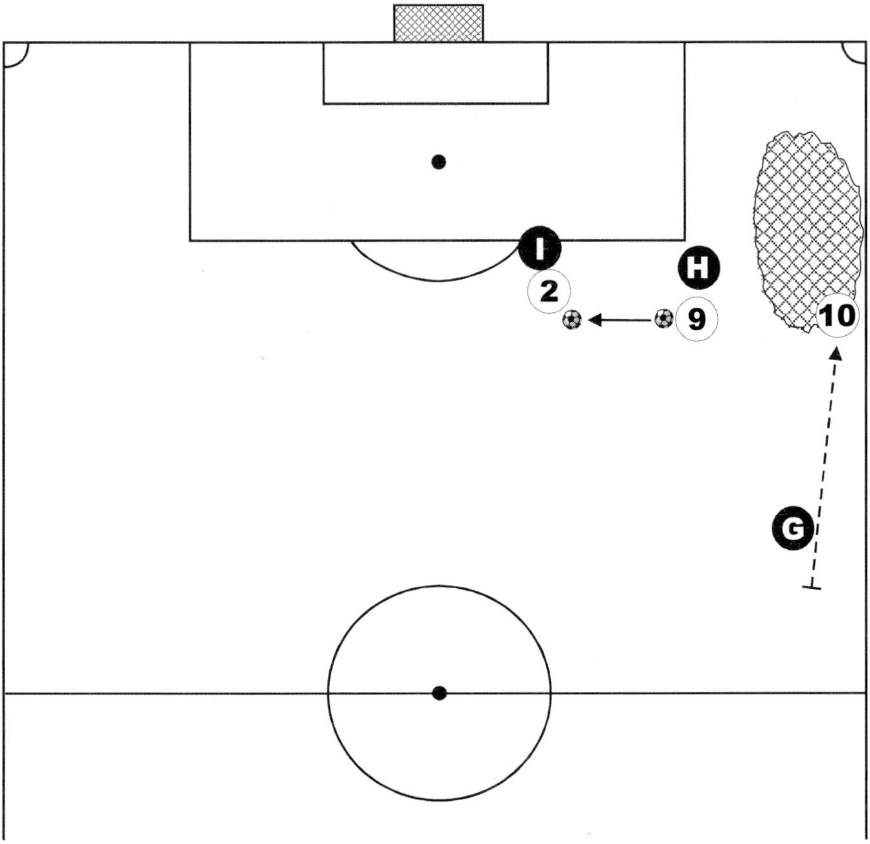

Diagram 9 - Player 9 has the ball and volley-passes it back to 2 (after receiving the ball, 9 can develop play - dummy movement - by screening H).
The movement of 9 is followed by his marking opponent, player H. This creates space for penetration by 10, who receives the ball from 2 and goes towards the end of the field to cross.

Paragraph C

Creating Space in Depth

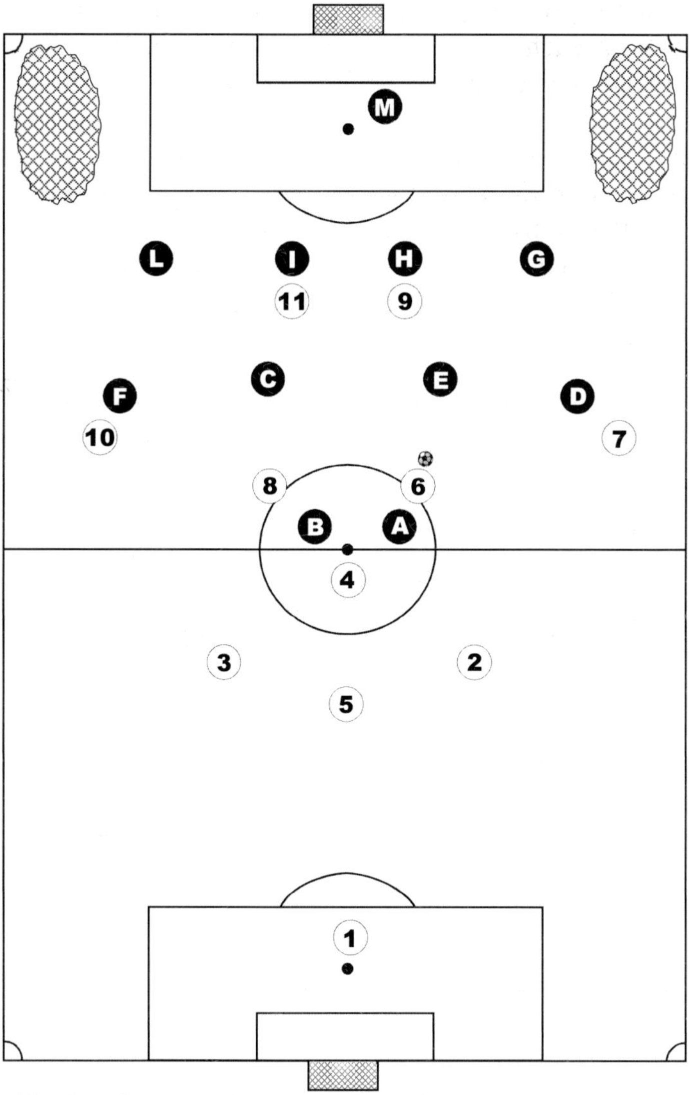

Diagram 10 - Creating space in depth on the wings through the movement of the two central attackers - double center-forward. The arrangement of the team with the ball is the 3-5-2, while the opposing team is arranged according to the 4-4-2.

N.B.: For coaching purposes only.

Let's consider the two arrangements shown in diagram 10.
In the attacking phase, in order to create and occupy space on the wings near the edges of the penalty area, I sometimes require the two forwards (in this case 9 and 11) to occupy the central corridor and to keep at a 5 to 7 yard distance from each other. This may seem inconsistent as the four opposing defenders would supposedly have an easier task both in marking and in covering.
Instead, thanks to the movement of 9 and 11 there can be:

1. a deep pass from 6 onto the wing where 11 runs to get the ball, thus eluding the off-side trap - possibly the defensive system applied by the four defenders - and getting into a position that enables him to have a clear vision of the ball, of his teammates, of the opponents and of the goal[2] as shown in diagram 11.

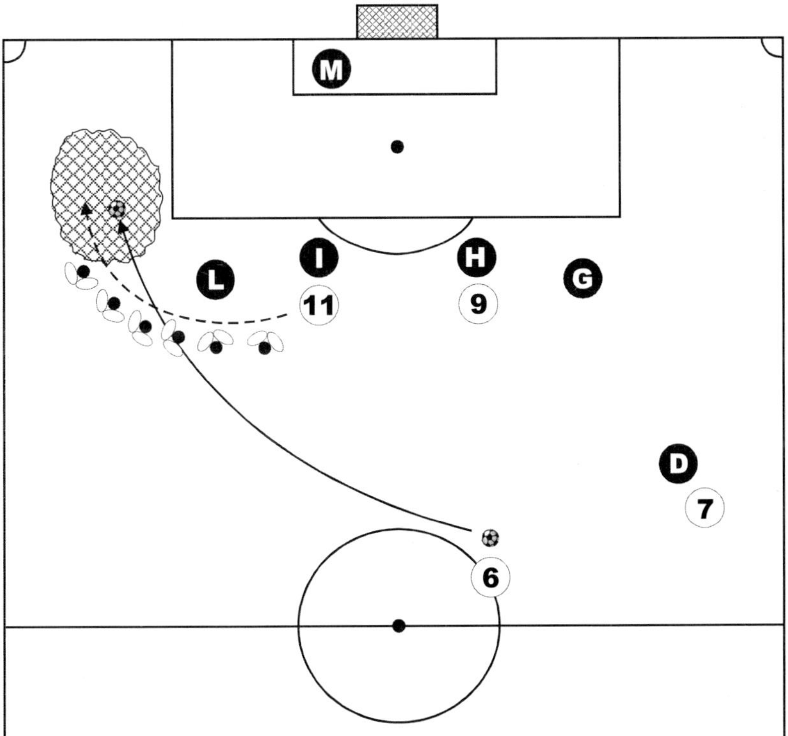

Diagram 11 - "Details": footwork, leg and body movement, eyes on the ball.

[2] This is what we recommend when playing a team with a man-marking arrangement: in such a case, take advantage of the speed of the forwards, also providing for their sudden criss-crossing.

2. 6 passes to 9 who moves diagonally, receives the ball and, pressured by G, passes it to 7 who penetrates (diagram 12).

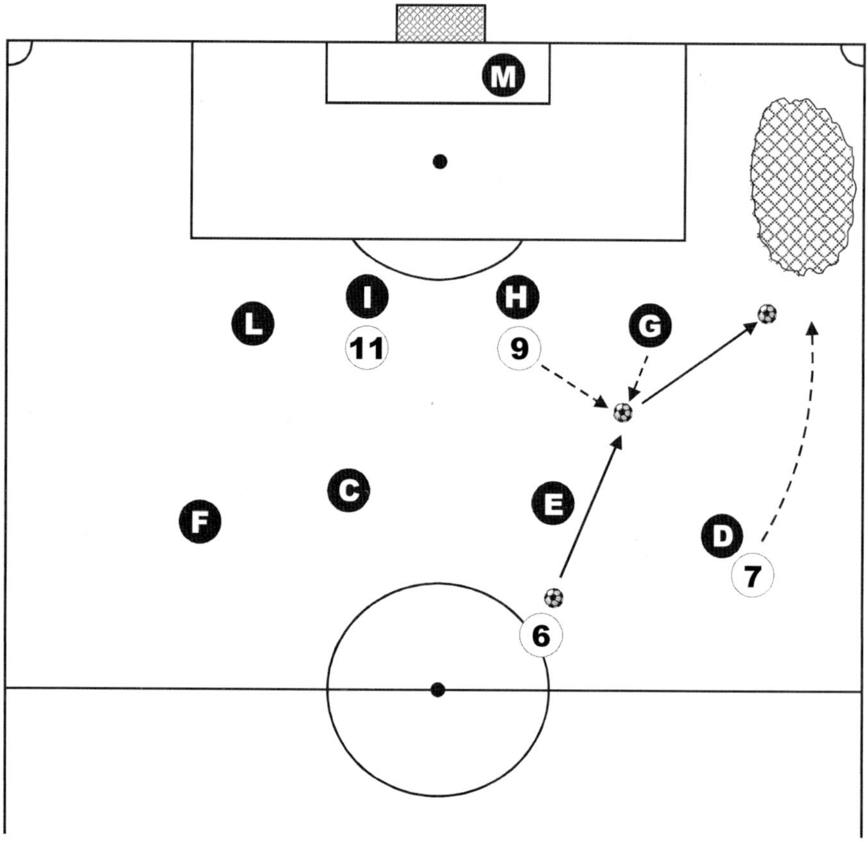

Diagram 12

Paragraph D

Building up the Play on the Wings - Search for Superiority in Numbers

- **Conditions:**
  - 4 players;
  - 3 opponents;
  - active goalkeeper.

First option:

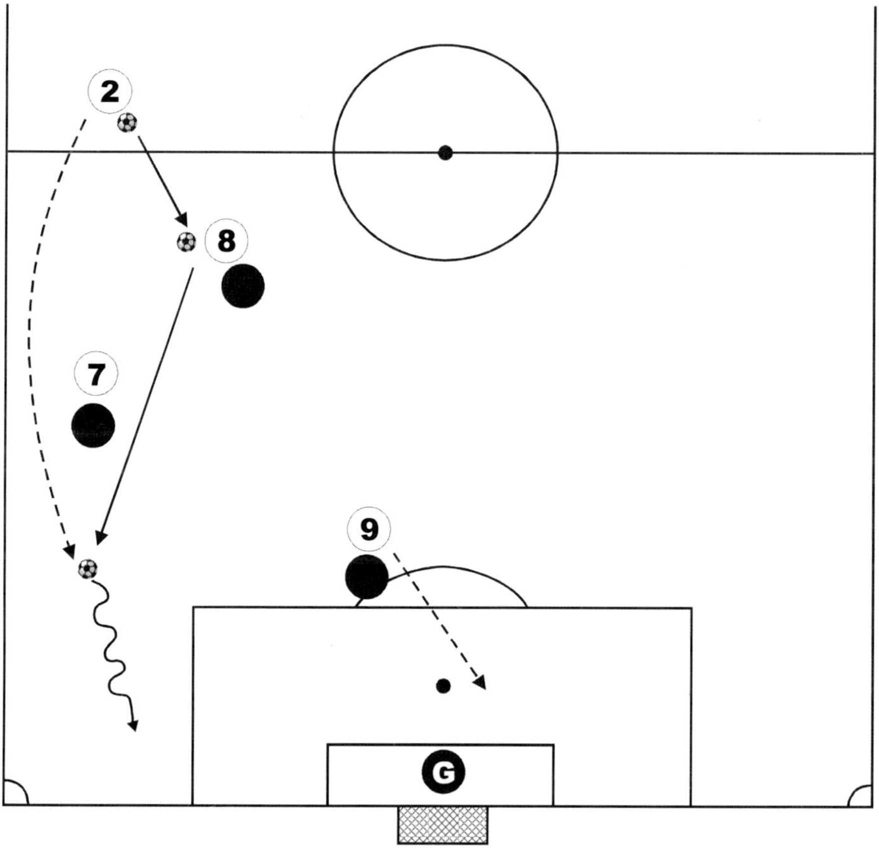

Diagram 13 - Player 2 passes the ball to 8, who is marked by an opponent, and then overlaps 7. Player 2 receives the pass back from 8, dribbles the ball to the end of the field and crosses to 9.

Second option:

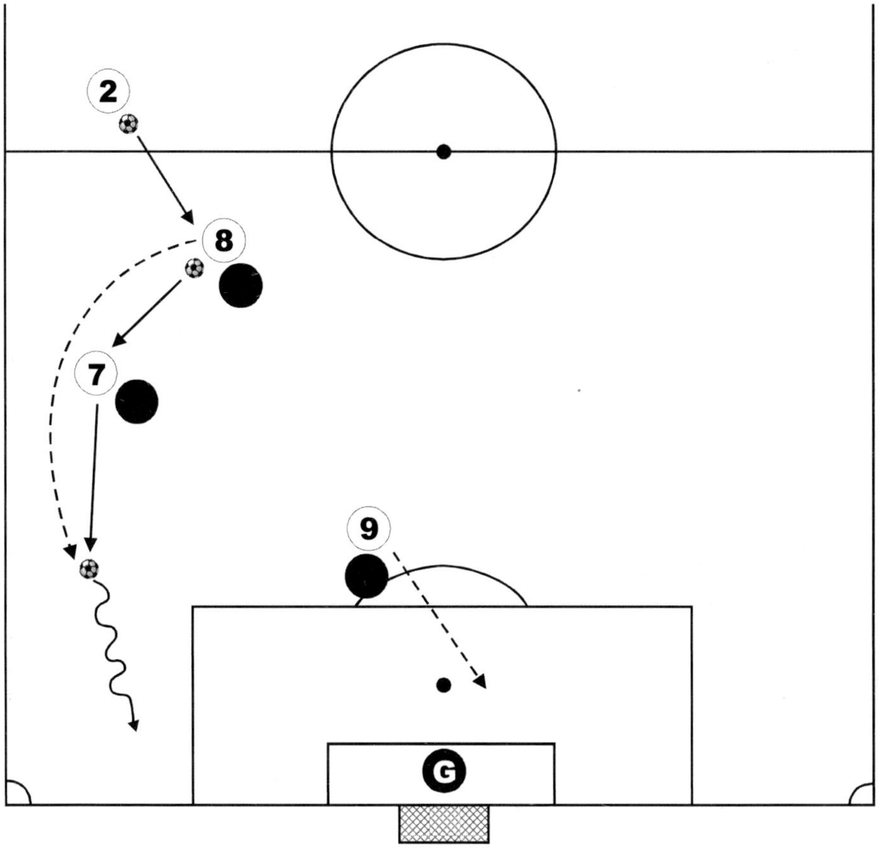

Diagram 13a - Player 2 passes the ball to 8, who is marked by an opponent. 8 passes it to 7 and then overlaps, receives the return pass, dribbles the ball to the end of the field and crosses to 9.

Exercise 1 - Phase A:

- ***Conditions***:
  - 4 players;
  - no opponents;
  - active goalkeeper.

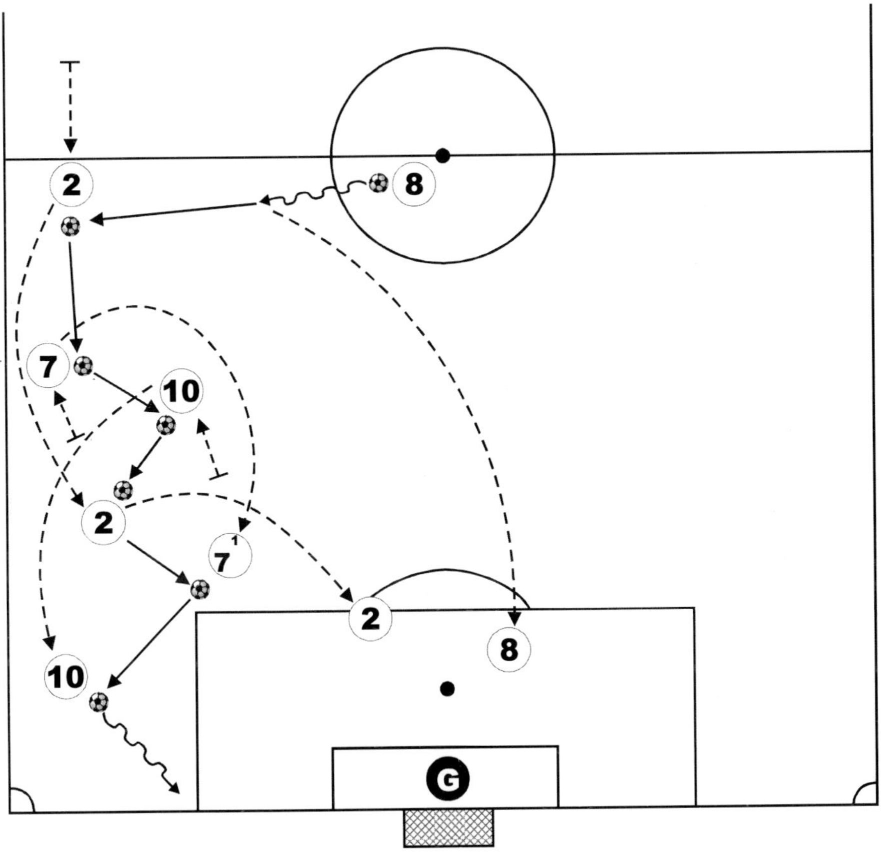

Diagram 14 - Player 8 dribbles the ball across the field and passes it to 2, who is coming from the back. Player 7 runs towards 2 and receives the pass, while 2 overlaps him. Player 7 sees the movement of 10 and passes him the ball, then runs to position 7^1. Player 2 receives the ball from 10 and passes it to 7^1, while 10 overlaps and then receives the ball from 7^1. Player 10 dribbles the ball to the end of the field and crosses to 2 and 8.

Exercise 1 - Phase B:

- ***Conditions:***
  - 4 players;
  - 3 opponents;
  - active goalkeeper.

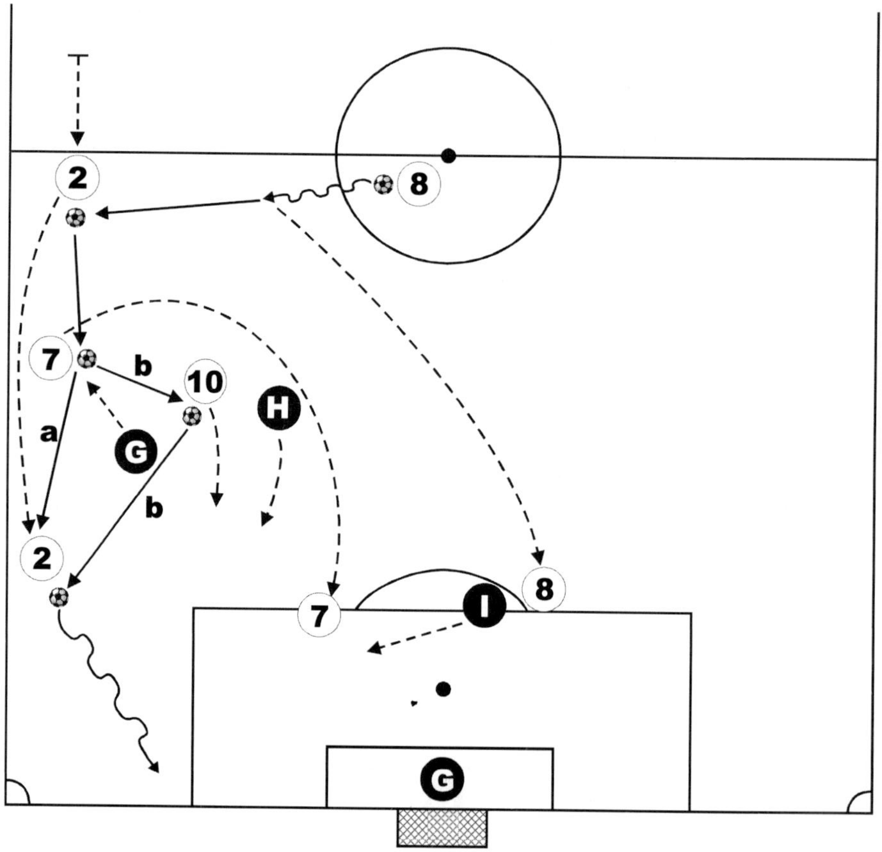

Diagram 15 - The same players shown in the previous exercise, with three opponents: they must find feasible and effective solutions that can give the team advantage.

Player 8 passes the ball to 2, who then passes it to 7, pressured by G. 7 has two options: he can either make a deep pass to 2, who is overlapping on the wing (option “A”), or he can pass the ball to 10 who then passes it to 2 on the wing (option “B”). Player 2 dribbles the ball to the end of the field and crosses to 7 and 8, marked only by opponent I. In the second situation (option “B”), when 10 passes the ball to 2, player 10 must be careful about both H’s defensive action and the off-side tactics which might be applied by I - in this case acting as a sweeper.

Another group of seven players carries out the same exercise on the left wing when the action on the right wing finishes.

In this way the coach has the time to correct and give focused advice to his players.

Exercise 2 - Search for deep play on the wings, cross from the end of the field:

- ***Conditions:***
  - 2 teams with 8 moving players;
  - 2 goalkeepers.

- ***Space:***
  it depends on the number of players.

- ***Aim:***
  in the four shaded areas shown in diagram 16 the players cannot be attacked

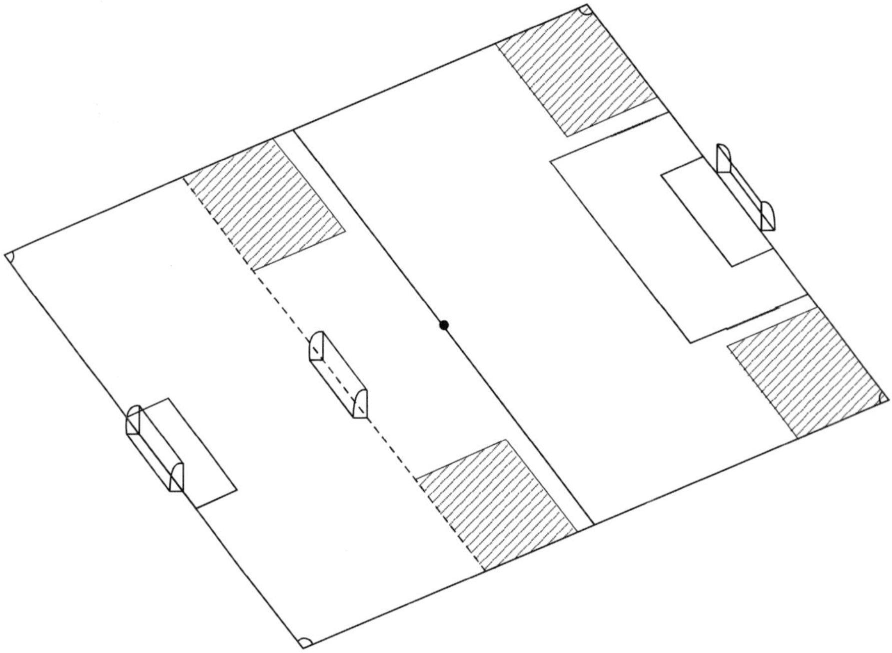

Diagram 16

Exercise 3 - Search for play on the wings, cross from the end of the field:

- ***Conditions**:*
  - 2 teams with 8 moving players;
  - 2 goalkeepers.

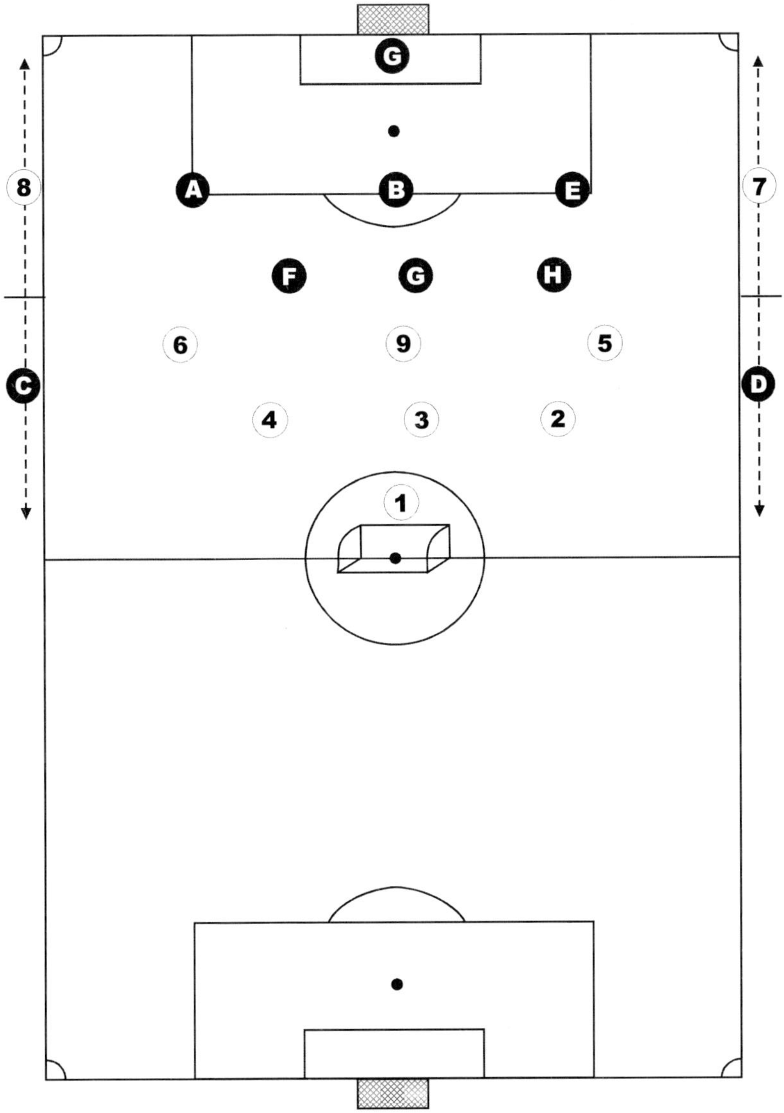

Diagram 17 - Each team has two players in the outside corridor, who take part in the game trying to cross from as close to the goal line as possible, without being attacked.
"Principle": "first time" crosses.

Paragraph E
Educational coaching

These exercises belong to what I call "educational coaching". It consists in submitting a situation to the players and making them solve it, like a problem at school. The player is in the field, and is faced with having to find a solution to the given situation.
This kind of work can also be done on a piece of paper or on a blackboard.
This kind of exercise enables the players to acquire and absorb, through neuro-muscular processes, the structural elements of the exercises[3].
The defenders are semi-active at first, then they become active in real time and pace of play[4].
One exercise of this kind is the so-called "shadow match": a team plays against 11 shadow players, who at first have an exclusively passive role. In this way the team gets more confident in the possession of the ball and in the development of play.

[3] I have noticed that in this way learning is faster and players develop a greater and steadier tactical awareness.
[4] These exercises are carried out with time and pace very similar to those of real matches.

PHASE OF NON-POSSESSION OF THE BALL

Paragraph F - Double-teaming

Double-teaming (or double-marking) is "a defensive tactical movement aimed at immediately winning possession of the ball or intercepting the pass".
While in the past it was carried out only by very few players, today it is typical of many clubs and national teams. In my opinion this "principle" is very important and I require my players to carry it out both on the wings and in the central zone of the field.
A defender tackles the opponent with the ball in front of him, while a teammate helps him by placing himself in such a way as to:
1) make the opponent's action difficult;
2) try to win possession of the ball when the opponent dribbles it to the inside (diagram 18).

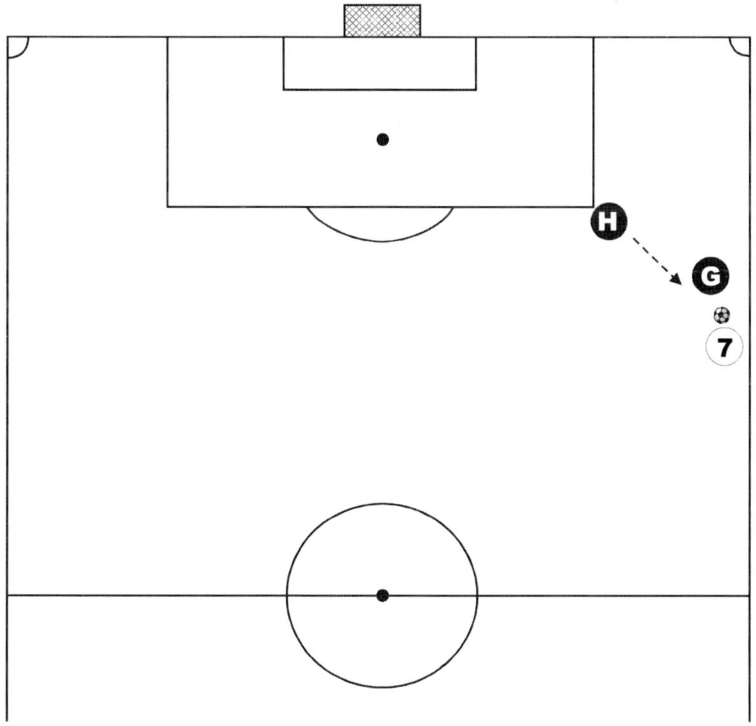

Diagram 18 - Rear Double-Teaming.

G tackles 7 trying to push him to the inside - the defender's "weak side" - in order to make H's action effective.
The same is required of midfielder E, who returns to double-team 7 as shown in diagram 19:

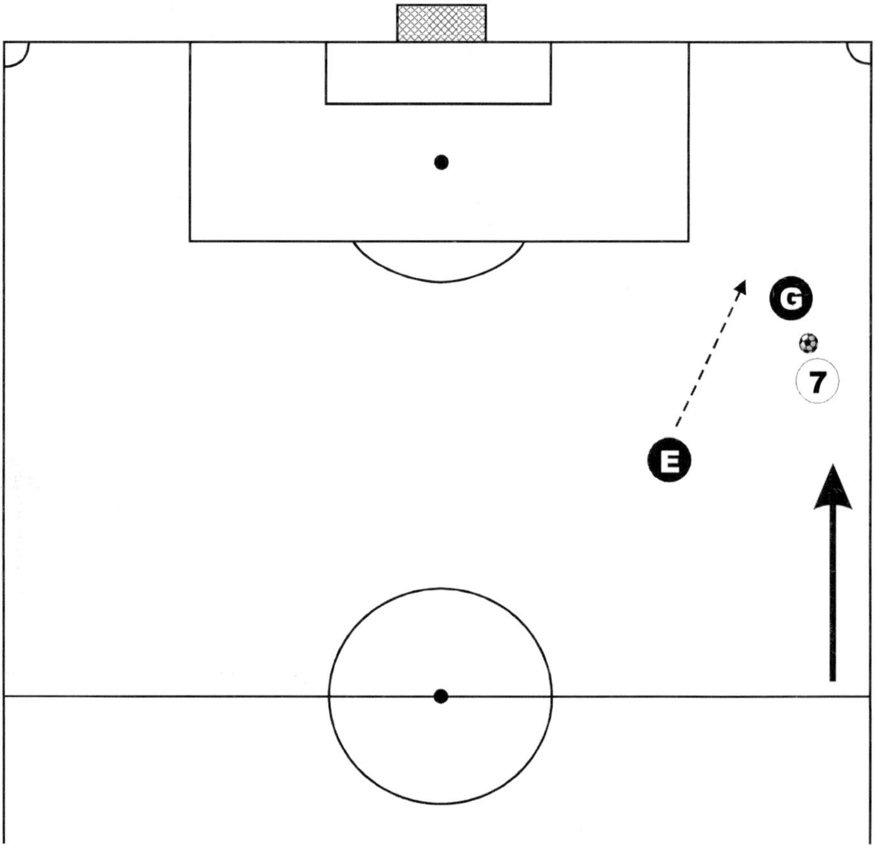

Diagram 19 - Rear Double-Teaming.

When player 7 (with the ball) has player G at his back, E must carry out a different movement: his main aim is to win possession of the ball with sideways double-teaming (diagram 20).

When 2 passes to 7, E double-teams 7 to steal the ball. His action will be effective because it will tend to reduce player 7's development of play.

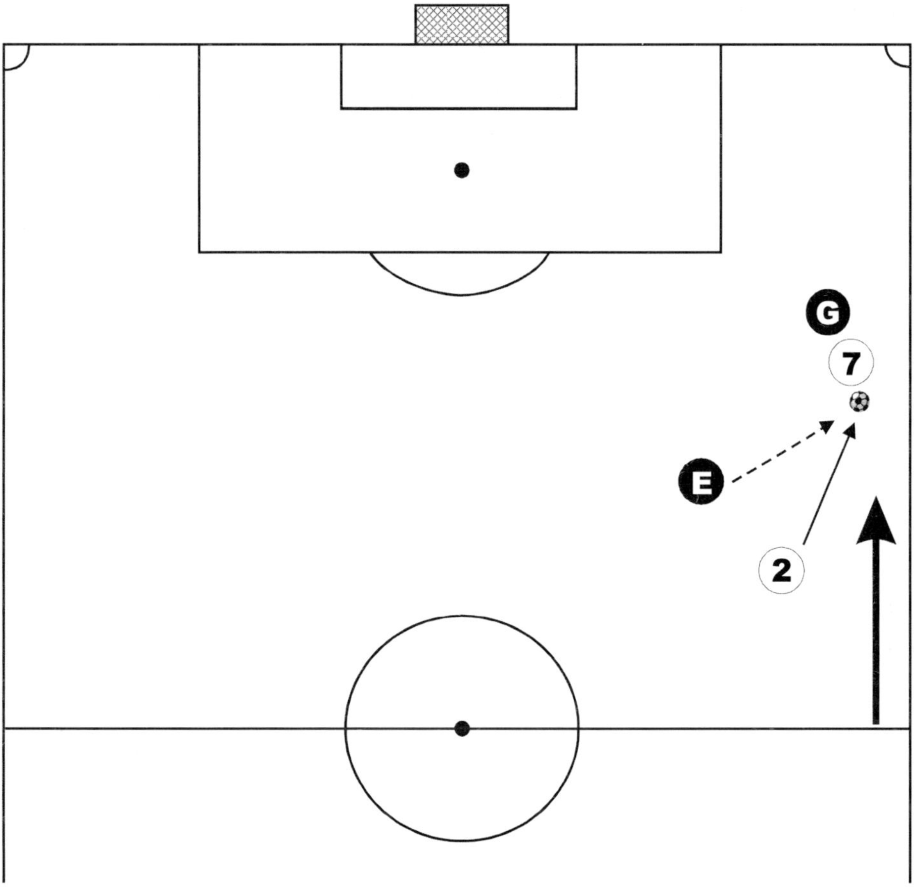

Diagram 20 - Sideways Double-Teaming.

Double-teaming aimed at winning the ball can be carried out all over the field. When carried out in the attack, it can be linked to pressure and be the prelude to an attack.
A pre-condition for double-teaming is that the distances between players must be short, particularly on defense.
Double-teaming requires tactical awareness, focus and timing. In fact, if applied hastily and instinctively, it may give way to fouls.

Therefore, coaching must include the objective of improving the **reflex activity** and the **motor response (reaction)** of the player involved in double-teaming.
Diagrams 18 to 20 show how double-teaming (both rear and sideways) is carried out from the technical point of view.
Coaching can start with groups of 4 players divided in pairs: for example, players 7 and 2 with the ball, G and H as opponents.
Their arrangement is shown in diagram 21 for **coaching purposes**:

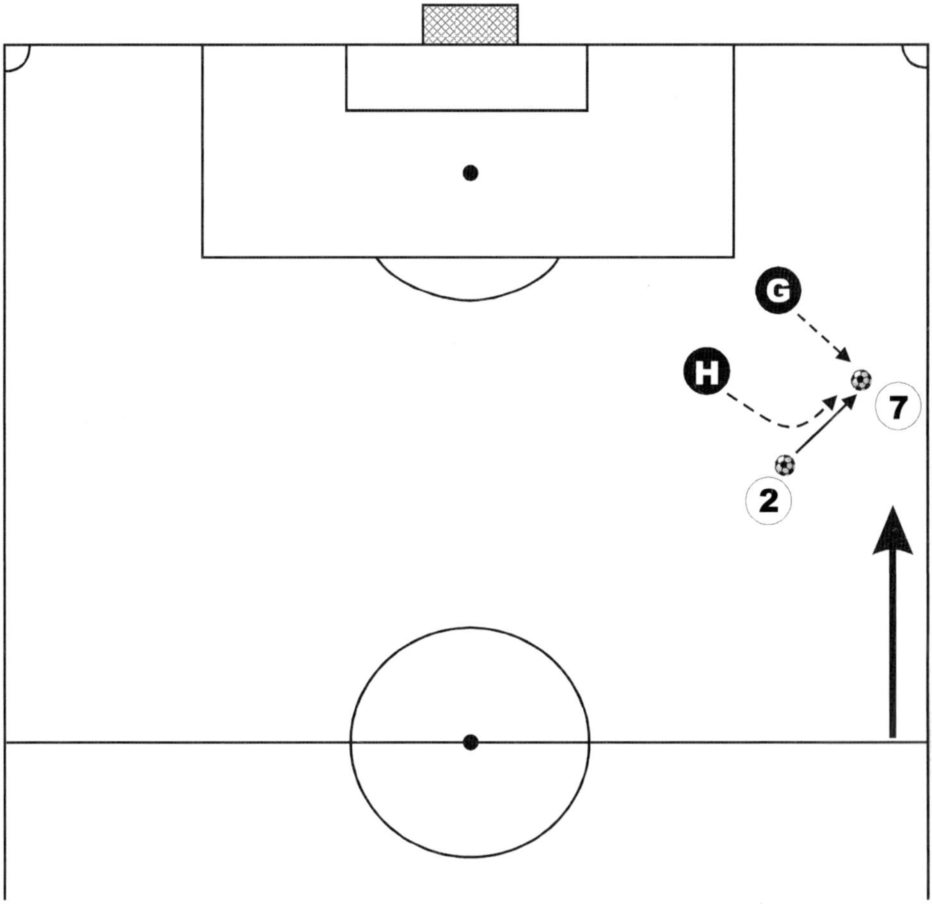

Diagram 21 - Player 2, with the ball, is challenged by H. He passes the ball to 7, who is marked by G. Player 7 tries to control the ball and dribble past opponent G. H modifies his run to double-team 7.

When double-teaming is carried out from behind the opponent there might be the risk of a foul due to the simultaneous challenge by the designated tackler and the double-teamer. Therefore, in this case the double-teamer must play for time (see diagram 18). Instead, the double-teamer intervenes before the designated tackler only if opponent 7 turns round to protect the ball (see diagram 20).

This exercise improves double-team tackling skills and also helps the players to find solutions in such situations. After passing the ball to 7 (double-teamed by G and H), 2 makes himself available for a deep pass as shown in diagram 22:

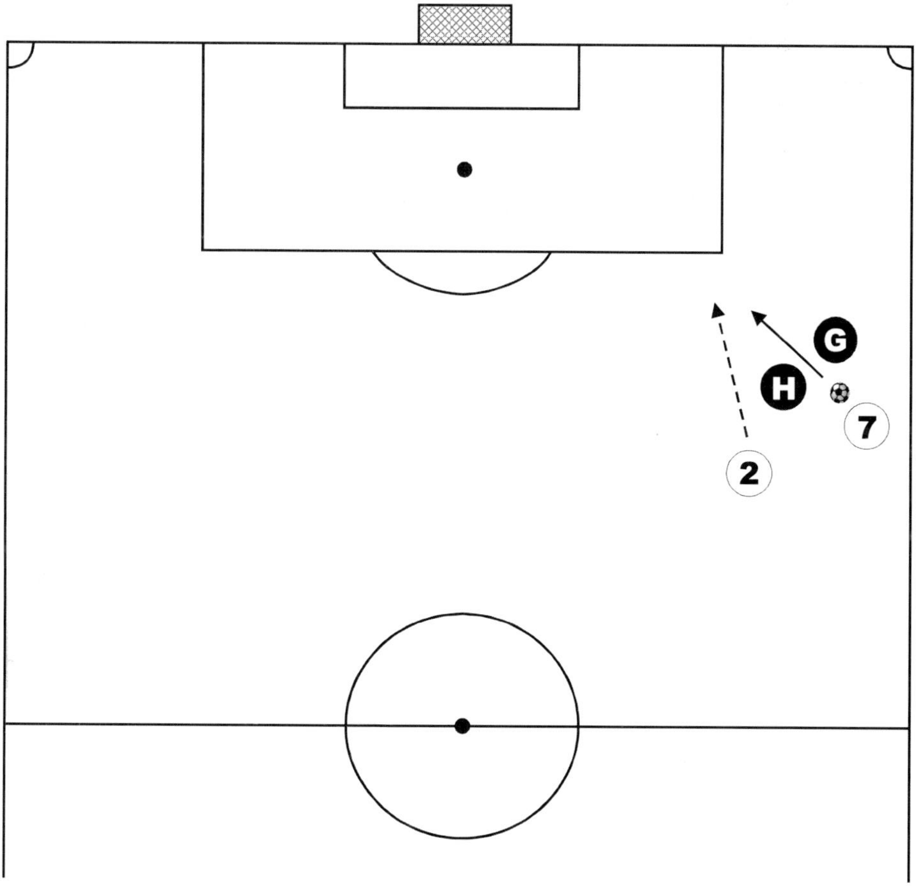

Diagram 22 - Making Oneself Available for a Deep Pass.
Player 7 can rely on 2, by passing 2 the ball before being tackled by G and H.

As I have said, sideways double-teaming is particularly important. It must be carried out with extremely accurate organization and timing, mostly with attackers and midfielders who can be helped by the sweeper who must prevent penetration in depth by an opponent. This exercise is carried out by six players divided into two groups, arranged in the central zone of the field. E, F and G are teammates and have the ball: they are arranged along a horizontal line, at a distance of 5-7 yards from each other. They are faced by opponents 9, 10 and 11 who are at 3-5 yards from them (in order to better simulate a real situation of play, see diagram 23).

Player E, with the ball, goes towards player 9.

At this point, player 10 has a key role: he must be in the right position and ready to intervene if his teammate is beaten. In order to make this cooperation simpler and safer, 10 can ask 9 (**tactical dialogue**) to close off the outside space, thus forcing the opponent to dribble the ball to the inside, where 10 will be ready to double-team. The same is required of 11.

These are the "tactical principles" of soccer. These exercises are extremely useful to train the team's movements to become automatic.

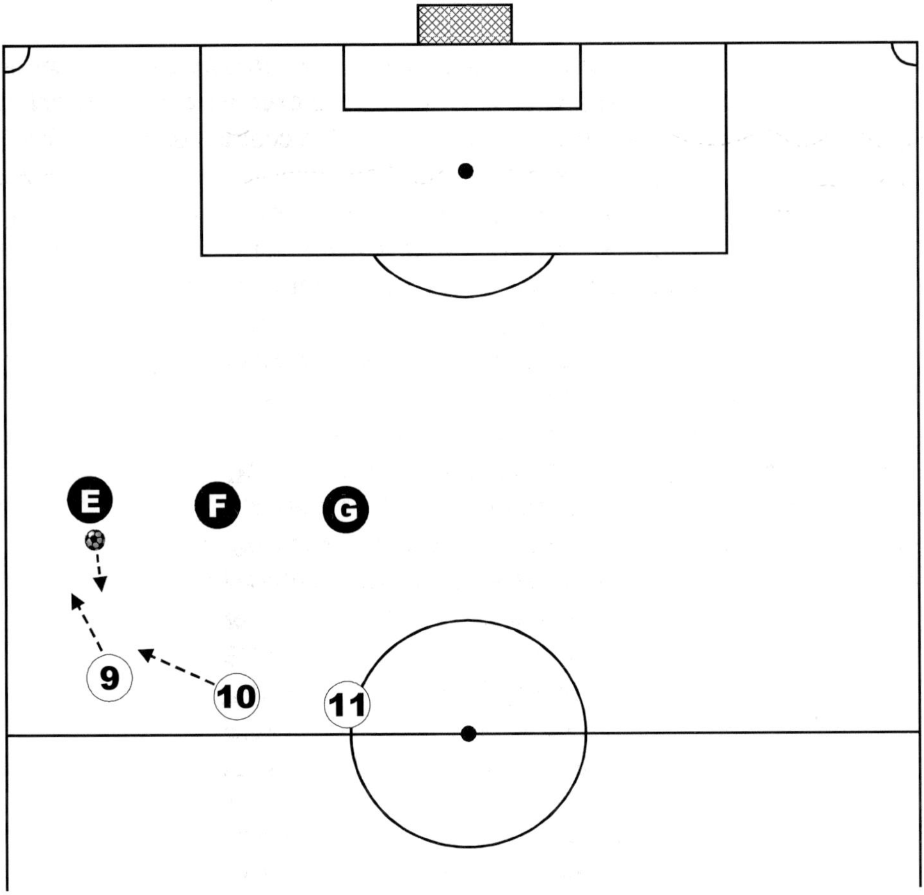

Diagram 23 - Player 10 gets ready to intervene on E, pushed to the inside by 9.

Tactical Dialogue - Verbal Communication

In today's soccer, the effectiveness of an action is also determined by verbal communication among players. Verbal communication is a "**fundamental skill**" in coordinating the movement of the players and the movement of the ball.

For example, the player who passes the ball tells his teammate what movement he should make: pass the ball forward, pass it back, protect it from a coming opponent, etc.

Paragraph G
Pressure - Counterpressure

The principles of pressure and off-side tactics are ascribed to Ajax and the Dutch national team (1970-1973).

These principles have undergone evolution. At first they were always combined and constantly applied. This quite often meant a fragmented kind of play, but the development and application of countermeasures have made them more rational and methodical.

Today many clubs apply these principles in a customized and flexible way, considering various factors. National sports culture, styles of play, the mentality of coaches, the skill of soccer players, and, last but not least, the application of concepts of coaching theory and of condition training methods are those elements which have mostly influenced the evolution of pressure and off-side.

From a technical point of view, the application of ***pressure*** means finding the answer to the following questions:

- Why and how does a team apply pressure?
- When, how deep and in what zones of the field should pressure be applied?
- What skills must the players have to be able to apply the off-side?

In the 4-4-2 and in the 3-5-2 all teams have given up man-marking, opting for a mixed kind of marking. In the 4-4-2, one of the four defenders acts as a "sweeper" in a shifting diagonal marking, while the others screen the opponent's points of reference. The failure of pressure applied in the attack or in the midfield makes one of the two central players shift diagonally to protect the defense from the opponent's possible long passes.

In the defensive phase, the 3-5-2 gives a better protection in case of mistakes, while in the attack it provides for a better balance between the attacking and the supporting players.
There are more teams which apply a "mixed" zone than those which opt for the so-called "pure" zone. The former show a more balanced protection and a more marked direct control on the opponents, while maintaining the principles for the attacking phases of play and the potential for scoring.

❑ Examples of pressure on a 4-4-2 arrangement (diagram 24)

The attack should always be carried out when the ball is close to the sideline. In this case the defender has only two options: either a long pass or a back pass. When shifting forward, the attack should be carried out on the wing: nine times out of ten there is an opportunity to steal the ball.

Diagram 24 shows, for coaching purposes only, just the actions of the three players in the front line.

The application of pressure needs maximum organization of the entire team, goalkeeper included. It is a strategy in which every player must know the general objective as well as the function of each member of the team.

"Pressure" is a group action in which all the players act at the same time, no matter how near or how far from the ball they are - it is the best expression of the idea of organization.

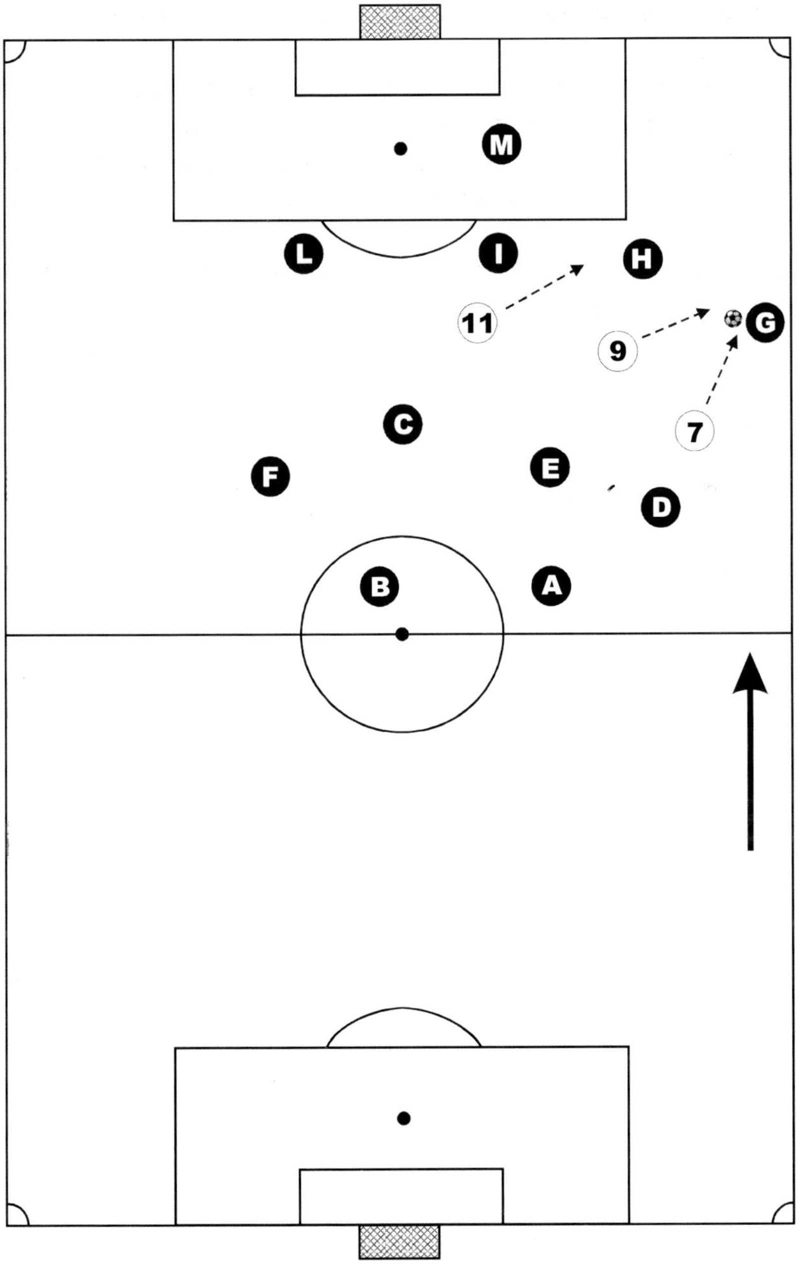

Diagram 24 - Pressure applied by the front line players.
Pressure applied by the three forwards: 7, 9 and 11.
7 applies pressure on opposing defender G.
9 applies pressure on the ball and the space.
11 applies pressure on the space between I and H.

"Hot action for cool minds". This is how I sum up the principle of pressure, the success of which is determined by players who are fit, quick, capable of physical endurance, skillful, intelligent, focused leaders, who demonstrate an explosive reaction (aggressive phase) once having accurately and with coolheadedness "read" the context of play.
I have used the educational and coaching exercises shown in the following pages to develop in my players an active and positive mentality and a cooperative and inventive attitude, resulting in a dynamic and effective kind of play under every playing condition.

Educational and Coaching Exercises

❑ Educational Exercises

I. "Torello" (one or more players inside a circle made up by other players must try to intercept their passes) with two players in the middle:

- **Restrictions:**

A. The players outside must play the ball with one touch only;
B. The players inside must play the ball with two touches, so that they are obliged to think before intervening;
C. The players must communicate verbally.

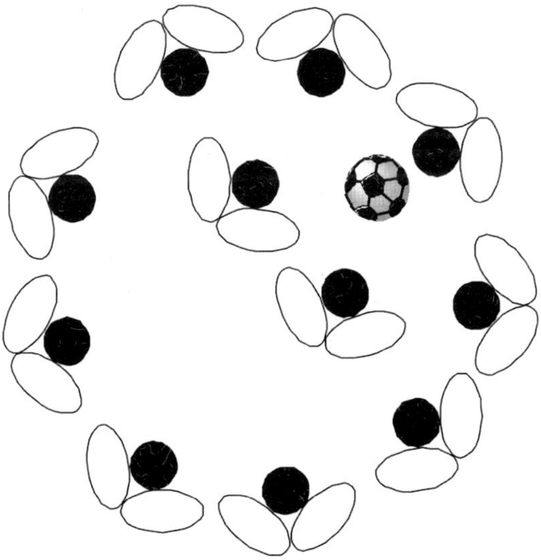

I. "Torello" with three players in the middle:

- **Restrictions:**

A. Pressure must be applied with one of the three players behind the two others;
B. The players outside can play the ball with one and/or two touches.

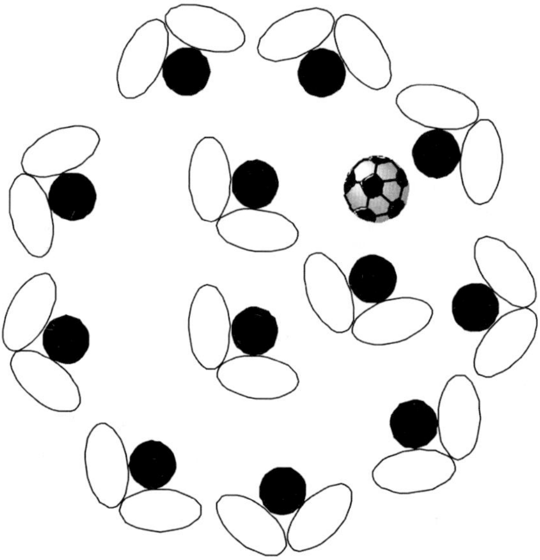

❑ Educational Exercises – specific for defenders

I. ***3 on 2;***

II. ***4 on 3;***

III. ***Space:***

A. in one half of the field;

B. marked by the prolongation of the side lines of the penalty area.

IV. ***Objective:*** the three defenders try to dribble the ball beyond the dotted line, hindered by the pressure applied by the two opponents.

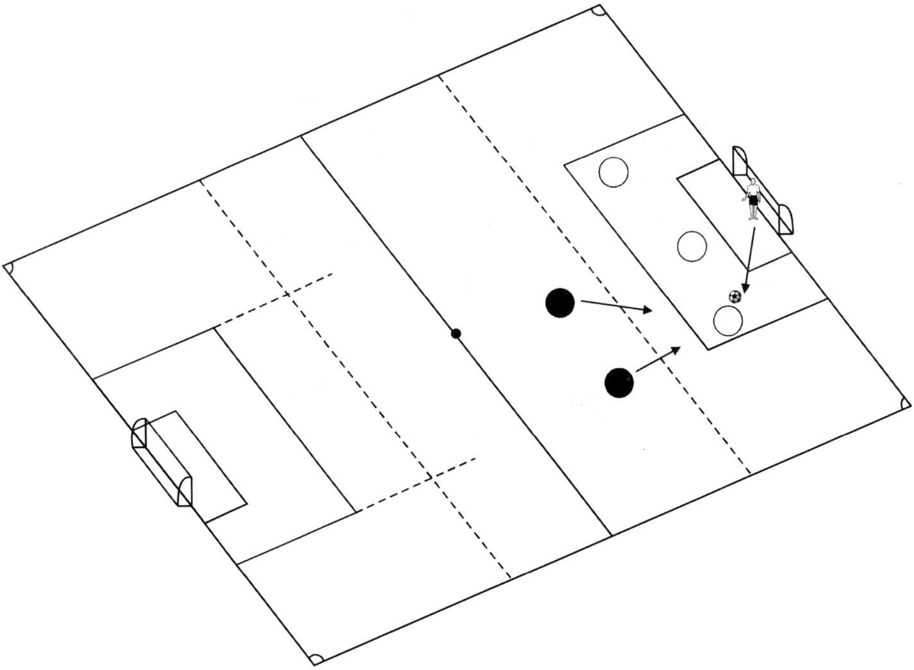

❑ Educational exercises

I. ***5 on 4;***

II. ***Space:***

a. marked by the dotted lines.

III. ***Objective:*** dribble the ball beyond the dotted line in the opponents' field.

N.B.: Every educational exercise can have a fundamental role for physical conditioning when carried out with maximum physical involvement and for longer than one minute.

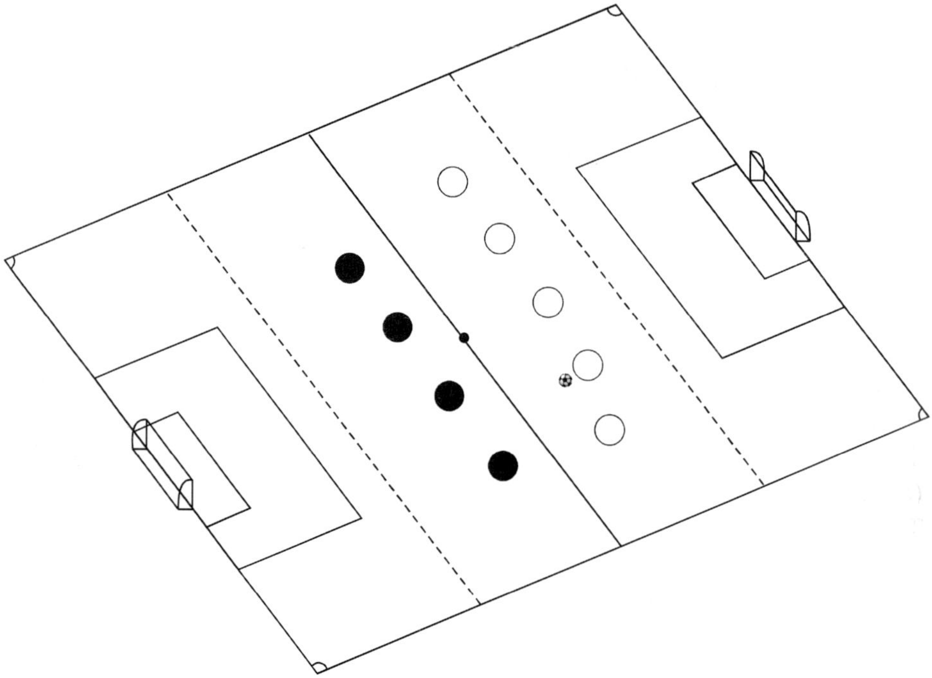

❑ Coaching exercise

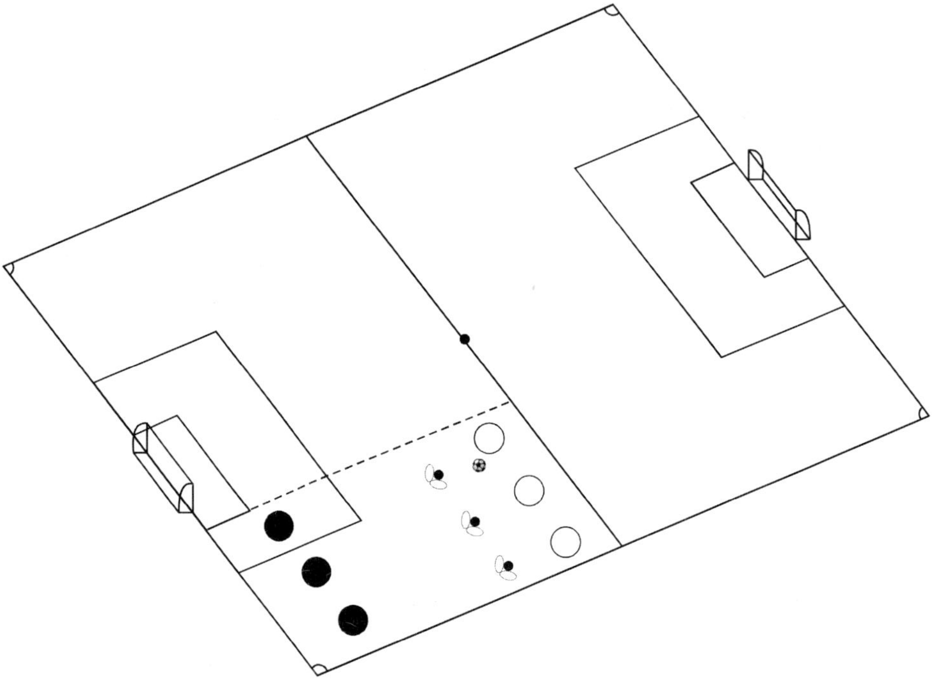

The three players whose orientation is indicated in the diagram apply pressure both on the players opposite them as well as on those at their back.
The ball is played as quickly as possible along the length of the field (about 55 yards).
The three "torello" players should practice for about one minute, then take a break.
Each group of three takes turns as "torello" players.

❑ Coaching exercise

I. ***8 on 8;***
II. ***Space*:** marked by the dotted lines;
III. ***At two touches***;
IV. ***Objective*:** dribble the ball beyond the dotted lines.

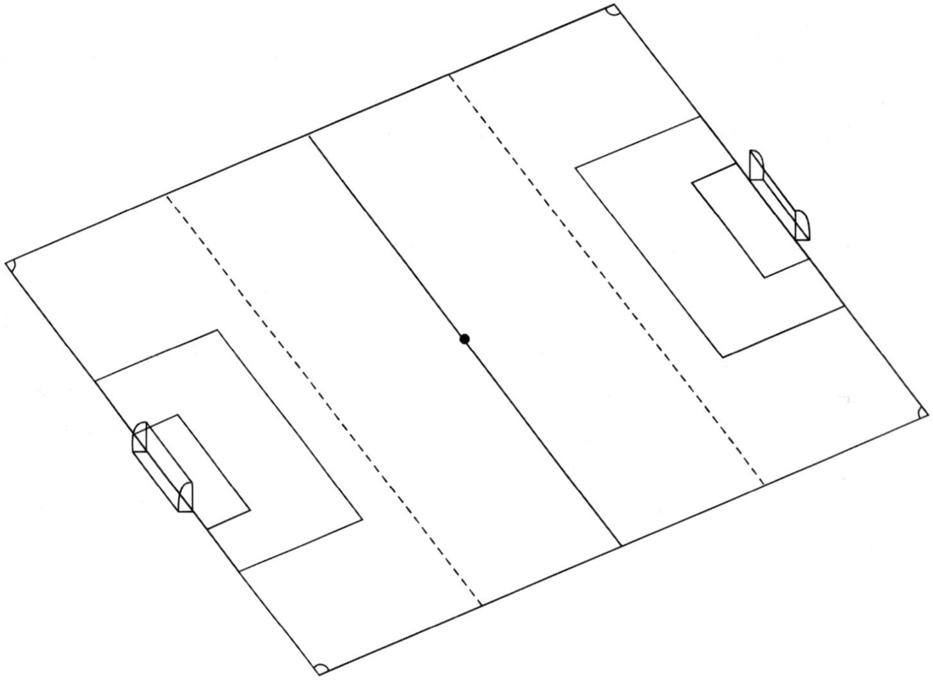

❑ Exercise

I. ***11 on 11****;*
II. ***Space:*** 35 x 35 yards
III. ***At two touches****;*
IV. ***Objective:*** a. dribble the ball beyond the lines;
b. develop "geometric" passes;
c. play against opponents;

N.B.: matches played at two touches on a smaller field lead to effective results.

The players must also be ready to undergo psychological pressure.
In fact, "pressure" aims at getting the player with the ball into trouble, making him pass the ball without reasoning and in an approximate way.
Coaching not only has technical-tactical objectives. It also helps the players to become self-confident and responsible for the choices they make. The players develop a mentality that helps them not to get discouraged when they lose the ball and to immediately react to win it back ("instant reaction ability").
Considering that, in today's soccer, "pressure" is a tactic carried out by many teams, I teach my team to take the initiative in order to limit the effectiveness of the "pressure" tactic.
The following are some such ***counterpressure*** initiatives:

- **prevent the opponent from getting organized** (defensive screen) When the goalkeeper returns the ball this can be done by kicking the ball over the midfield through long passes to the forwards, challenged by the defenders. If the ball is lost in the tackle it is not a big problem: the team is already 30-40 yards forward and in place. From this point of view, I get my players accustomed to making passes to the chest of the forward. In aerial challenges, the forwards are expected either to win the ball or to apply pressure on the opponent's clearance and if they win the ball (a 50% chance) they can play on wider and freer spaces, 30 yards forward in the attack, with fewer problems.
- **always have a player ready to cover**
- **make the goalkeeper play as a sweeper**
- **quick ball**: the ball must always be moving and passed with quickness (one-two combinations), to break through the opponents' lines
- **sudden counterattack with deep passes to narrow corridors**
- **agreements between two or more players** (verbal communication in that context)

Paragraph H
The Off-side Tactics

The “off-side” tactic could be the final phase of a “pressure” movement carried out by all the players of a team behind the line of the ball, and can enable the ball to be won back
1. by a free-kick,
2. by aggressive pressure.

If the “off-side” is applied systematically, then it is likely to cause mistakes or give a chance to the opposing team to find adequate countermeasures: in fact, in the past some teams would leave 30 yards between the goalkeeper and the last defender, but they were regularly beaten in the quarterfinals or semifinals.

Holland and Belgium were the national teams which invented this kind of “off-side tactic”.

It is important to analyze the “off-side” according to three parameters: where, how and when to apply it.

Today, the space between the defenders - who do not shift forward any more - and the goalkeeper, tends to be reduced, so as to result in a better organized team. In fact, if the ball goes towards the wings, the defenders are ready to intervene. Alternatively, if the ball filters past the defenders, the goalkeeper has a good chance to win it (see diagram 25).

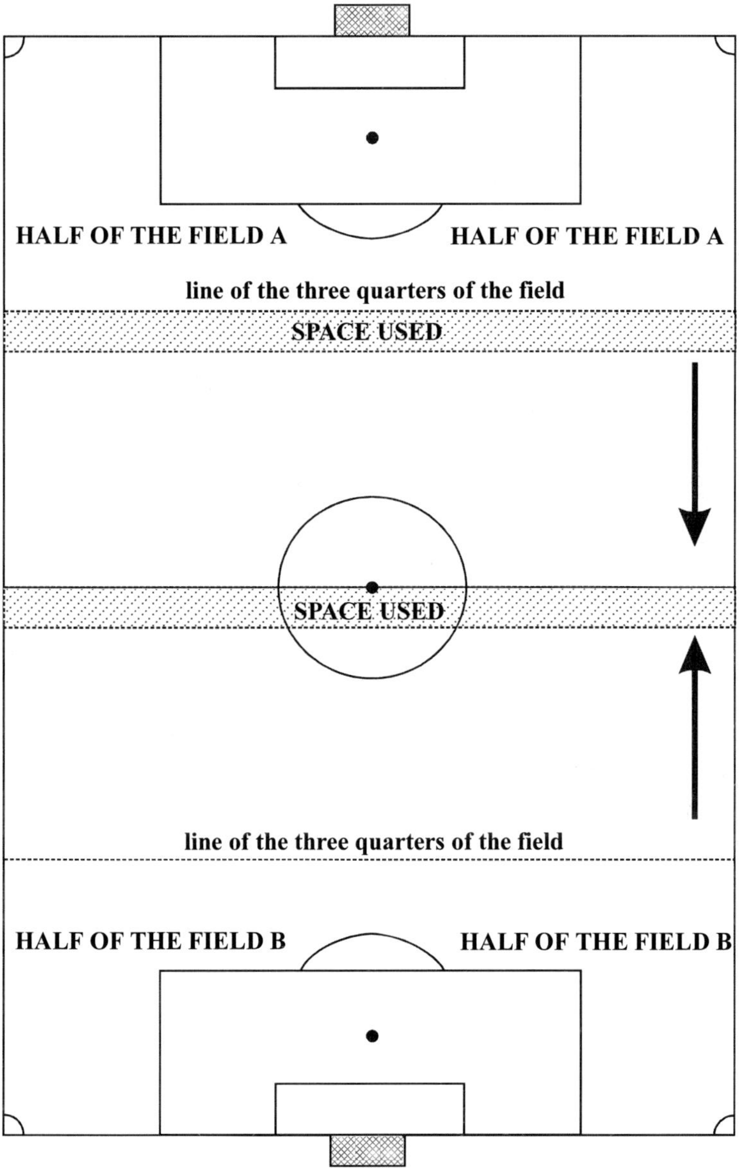

Diagram 25 - Evolution of the "off-side" tactics.
Half of the field B: space used to apply off-side with a considerable distance from one's own goalkeeper.
Half of the field A: space used to apply off-side with a shorter distance from the goalkeeper.

In this way the opponent cannot go on a solo run towards the goalkeeper and the defender has an opportunity for not getting a red card - as last defender - if he fouls him.
The off-side can also be applied through defensive pressure: the sweeper moves forward towards the ball, leaving space control and cover with the two central backs.

Chapter 2

Positions and Their Technical-Tactical Evolution

- Foreword
- The goalkeeper
- The sweeper
- The central backs
- The side or wing midfielders
- The central midfielders
- The attackers - the forwards
- Playing in the air
- Passing - "Geometric" passing
- A more offensive soccer
- Exercises
- How to find space in pressure situations involving throw-ins

Foreword

In today's soccer, a player must improve both in the defensive and in the offensive phase in order to reach a positive performance.
The ever-growing application of "zone", or "mixed-zone" patterns, makes team performance a more important objective than individual performance and requires everyone's involvement.
The three points awarded for victories in professional soccer and the performance objectives have created a flexible player who cannot be defined by traditional soccer parameters.
Flexibility is therefore the quality to be constantly improved.
Today's high performance player must always be ready to do his best in any context of play (attacking or defending) or space (wings or central zones), from the technical-tactical (ball and situation), psychological and cognitive (leadership and intelligence) points of view.
He must be able to read and understand the phase of play, and at the same time, react with appropriate adequate motor movements.

The Goalkeeper

For many reasons, this role has undergone major evolution: better gear (glove and protective materials), scientific discoveries, better shooting skills and exploitation of set play situations, zone arrangement of teams applying pressure and off-side tactics, and new rules.
The goalkeeper's area of action is not only the penalty area - where he can use his hands - but it has extended to the space outside it, where he is limited to using his feet.
Very often he plays as a sweeper: he supports the defenders who back-pass the ball to him. He is ready to intercept the opponent's deep penetrating passes and he must frequently tackle the opponent who has dribbled past the last defensive line. Sometimes he also starts attacks.
Therefore, he must improve his kicking skills, develop good control and feel for the ball, self-confidence and adequate skills both in short and long passes to pass over the midfield line. Position-targeted coaching must be carried out starting from the youth level in order to have a player with good hand and foot skills.
The goalkeeper has had to evolve his positioning too, moving, for example, from the far post to the near one when, on corner-kicks, the ball does not have a spin, but is kicked with strength and precision towards the space in front of the near post, from which another offensive player can nearly always score.

The Sweeper

In traditional soccer the sweeper "covered" all the defenders, in particular the "stopper" (who man-marked the opposing center-forward) with whom he had to establish a good understanding when they "switched" the marking. He was considered the last defensive "line" and he did not really take part in building up the play.
Instead, today's tactical patterns have changed his position, lining him up with the other defenders. However, when a team does not apply the "off-side tactics" the sweeper is always ready to position himself behind the other defenders to cover the space at their back.
On defense, the sweeper's functions have remained unchanged, no matter the pattern of play.
There has, however, been an evolution in his role when his team is on offense: he can become the first player to build up play. If he is good at making long and accurate passes (*as we can often see in English soccer)* he can enable a teammate to go and shoot at goal, he can build up schemes in the midfield play and reach the opposing half of the field and shoot (finalizing action).
The "sweeper", sometimes called "central defender", must have good fundamental skills and be good at tackling, marking and aerial play, and he must also be physically strong and quick.
His tactical skills and sense are vital. He must be able to read the play, anticipate the situation and choose both his position and when to delay or tackle the opponent. He must be experienced and have a strong personality, convey confidence to his teammates and be a point of reference for everybody, both on and off the field.
He is usually a leader for his team.

The Central Backs

They must be "able to mark" the opponent when he gets into their zone.
When the opponent does not have the ball they must prevent him from receiving it and anticipate him. They must man-mark him when he gets the ball with his back to the goal. The defensive action is effective when the opponents cannot turn around and are obliged to play the ball in a less dangerous area.
The main characteristics of the central backs (sometimes called "central markers") are their physical strength, aerial power, determined tackling skills, intelligent aggressiveness, good timing, clear vision, ability to cover and support a teammate in trouble, self-sacrifice and responsibility.
Besides, as these players move and play in the central zone or "shooting area" in front of the penalty area, they must be careful not to cause free-kicks. Otherwise, opponents with good shooting skills and valid schemes could easily score a goal.

The Side or Wing Midfielders

Today's soccer uses the definition "side player" for those roles that in traditional soccer were called "offensive back", "linkman", "wing".
In the 4-4-2 zone pattern and in the 3-5-2 mixed zone there are usually two kinds of side players whose task is mostly to cover and use the wings according to the wing where they play better.
In the 4-4-2 the two side defenders must have more defensive abilities: man-marking - anticipate, tackle, not let themselves be beaten in the one on one - and zone marking, covering the field in diagonals, double-teaming, supporting the defensive line by covering the outside spaces in pressure situations.
When their team has the ball, these players participate in the attack by supporting the midfielders and the attackers, penetrating and making themselves available in the free spaces in the wings, in order to quickly cross or shoot at goal.
The functions of the side defender are the same as those of the side midfielder, but the latter must have more attacking technical-tactical skills: the ability to dribble fast (beat the opponent in one on one situations, break away from the defensive screen - ***inestimable value***), and, while running, make accurate cross-passes from any position, especially from near the end of the field, in order to provide for a wider play and a wider front to the attack, as shown in the 5-3-2.
Especially in the 4-4-2, these two players must have a perfect understanding between themselves, both in the defense and in the offense: they must be complementary, have good timing and be an extremely flexible pair.

The Central Midfielders

Today's central midfielder has all those functions that traditionally were attributed to defensive midfielders, playmakers and attacking midfielders. He mostly covers central corridors: he must be responsible for the team's balance and be able to read the play both to support the defensive action (ability to intercept and steal the ball) and to see his teammates' movements and availability in the attacking phase.

His fundamental tactical skills are a strong sense of position, tactical insight and anticipation of the development of play. From the technical point of view he is a steady player who can use either foot very well, with a gift for "geometric" play and schemes, confident both in short and long passes and in shots from far out.

The athletic skills required for this position have evolved remarkably. In fact, those who play in the middle of the field move and act more than all the others, both from a qualitative and quantitative point of view.

Until some years ago the central midfielder was mainly required to have strength, power and endurance. Today's more dynamic and aggressive soccer also requires him to be agile, reactive and quick.

One midfielder which is difficult to place and manage in today's soccer is the so-called "creative player". He is an atypical player endowed with good skills, inspired and creative, able to make unpredictable moves and to assist the attackers. However, he is a "flair" player, has scarce self-sacrifice and does not have a bent for defending. The coach must use this player practically and effectively. He should place him in a pattern with adequate schemes in order to enable him to develop the play according to his potential without jeopardizing the team's tactical and psychological balance.

The Attackers - The Forwards

The most praised soccer player is certainly the effective striker. He is characterized by his ability to shake off a marker and make himself available, the ability to always "see" the goal and the feel for scoring; he must have good elevation, be powerful, good at acrobatic play, clever and opportunistic. These qualities, typical of such a role in traditional soccer, today are no longer enough. In fact, zone patterns, pressure, off-side, double-teaming, higher pace and continuous attack reversals, have transformed the role of this position and adapted it to current play requirements, both in the offensive and defensive phases.

When the team has the ball he participates in building up the action, creates and makes free spaces for his teammates' penetration, makes himself available for deep passes, goes towards his teammate who has the ball (to support him), makes himself available for one-two passes, is deft and versatile in quick play and schemes.

As he plays in narrow spaces and is pressured by the defenders, he needs to have outstanding technical-tactical and psychological skills.

In the defensive phase, he is the team's first defender. He tries to block the beginning and the development of the offensive action, applies pressure, double-teams and tries to intercept the opponents' possible back passes.

When there is a set play situation (corner kicks or free kicks) he takes up a pre-established position in the penalty area. If necessary and required by the coach, he can help the team on other occasions too.

A good scheme for the two forwards is shown in diagram 26.

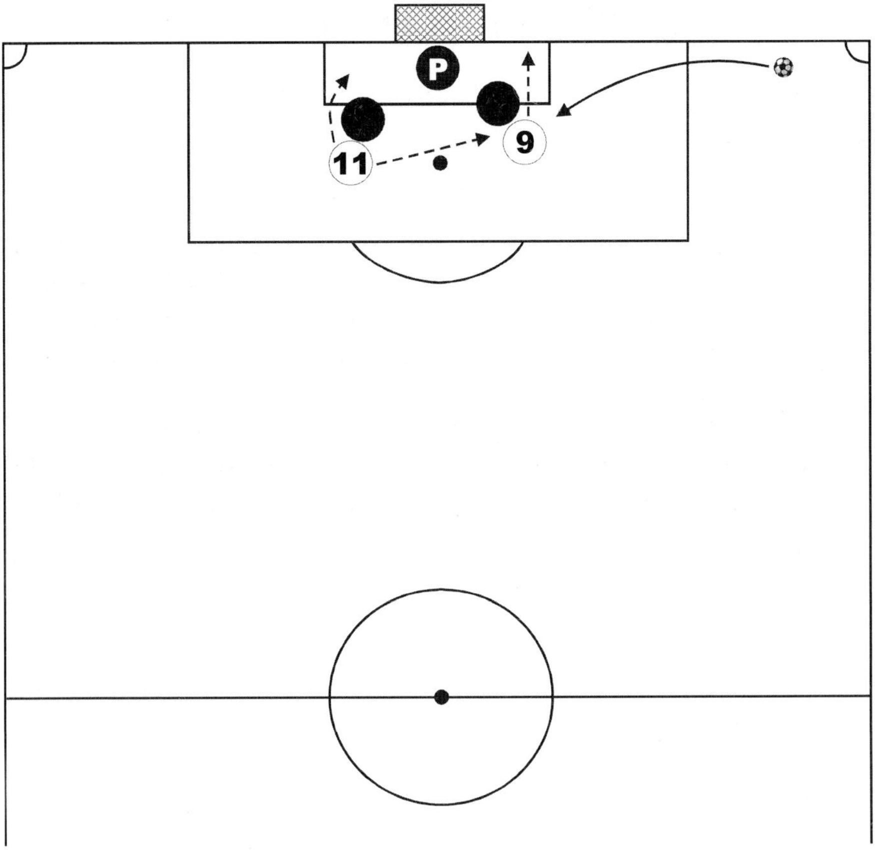

Diagram 26 - Movement of the two forwards when there is a cross from the end of the field.

When there is a cross from the end of the field I recommend the following movements: 9 moves to the near post followed by the opposing marker (a movement that gets the goalkeeper into trouble). 11 feints to go to the far post and goes towards the ball with a little advantage with regard to his marker, setting the stage for a shot at goal.
"Details" to work on: volley-kick, vision, synchronism, timing, body movement, leg movement and elevation.

Playing In the Air

Two aspects to pinpoint:

1. balance in elevation;
2. accurate performance of elevation.

It is important to know on what foot the player takes off: if he is right-handed he takes off on his left foot, and on the right foot if he is left-handed. If players are not coached to take off on either foot without distinction, defenders in particular will meet difficulties when the ball comes from the opposite side.

Therefore it is necessary to develop foot support and acquire balance in the take-off and aerial phases, both to hit the ball as effectively as possible and to ensure personal safety, given the physical contact and challenge with the opponents.

Passing - "Geometric" Passing

Passing is the fundamental technical skill[5] in every phase of play. In every coaching session I pay particular attention to all its details: passes must be simple, quick and accurate in order not to get one's teammate into trouble and not to allow the opponent to anticipate, double-team or apply pressure. Therefore, control, feel for the ball, command and self-confidence with the ball in pressure situations must be improved. 6 on 3, 5 on 2, 4 on 2 small sided exercises give good results in developing these skills.

Psychokinetic exercises[6] stimulate two important aspects: safety in immediate passes and the ability to play with one's head up.

Command of ball control and dribble enable a player to have better and wider vision, so that when the player gets the ball he is already in a position to play it. Such command is the answer when the action does not develop through long deep passes, or horizontal or diagonal passes aiming at switching the play, but through passes in the midfield (even for long periods of play). In this case I make use of the so-called "geometric" passing (**geometry is extremely important in high performance soccer too** - Editor's note). When the midfielders are pressured and cannot turn around and dribble, the ball must travel along "triangles" until a solution for forward play is found (see diagram 27).

The following scheme has been conceived **for coaching purposes only**: the ball is passed by the goalkeeper to 8 and then it reaches 2 through geometric passes; 2 develops the action further by passing the ball to the free space for 10's penetration.

[5] The most important skills are of course those one cannot do without, but they also include those that enable a team to strategize the score leading to positive results.

[6] Those phases that lead from perception to choice, in ever-growing rapidity, enabling a positive response to today's soccer requirements.

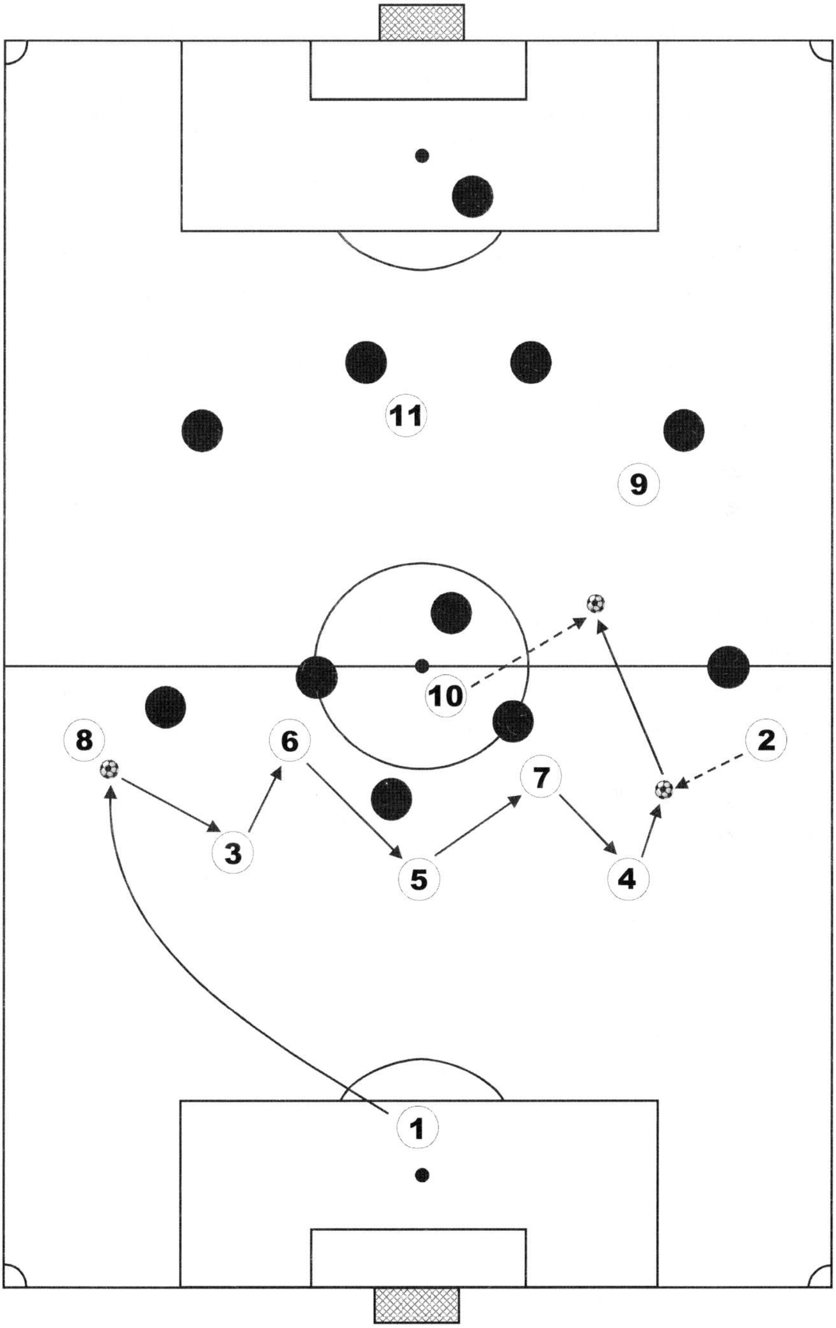

Diagram 27 - Development of play: geometric passing. Ajax' scheme.

It is very important to improve the speed and accuracy of passing. Simple exercises like the ones shown in diagram 28 can be useful in making the movement automatic, thereby achieving effective results.

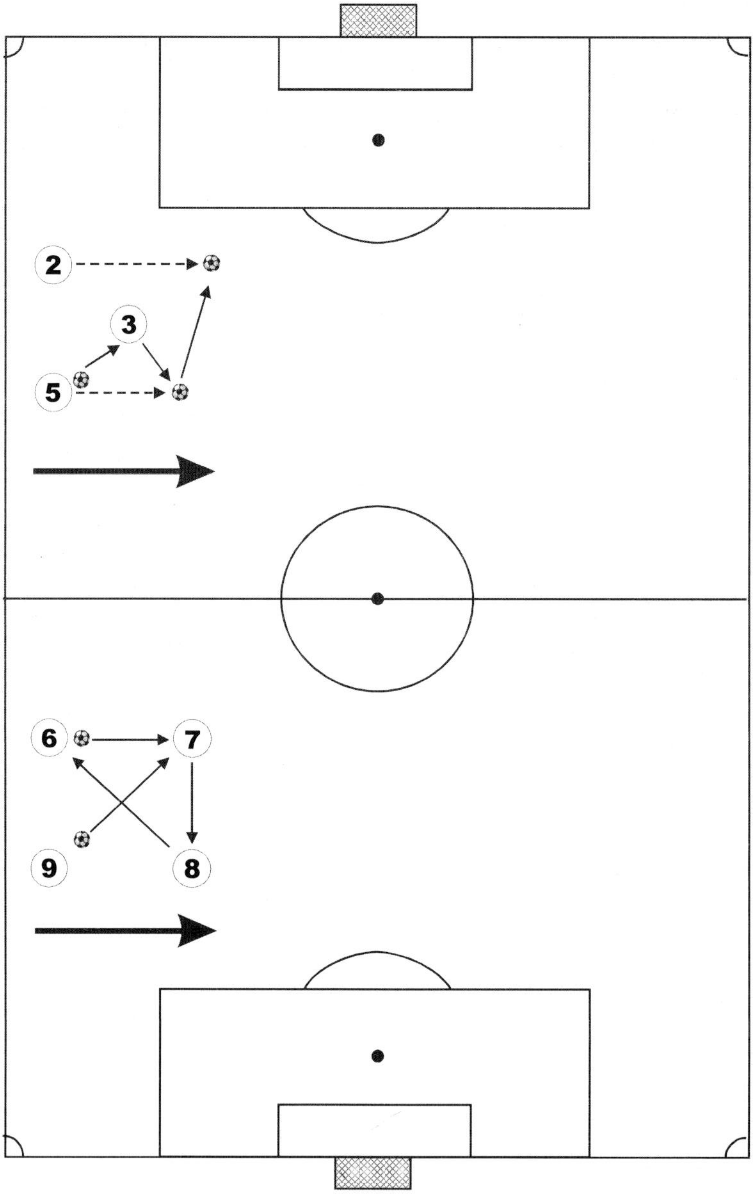

Diagram 28

In threes or fours, the players make level passes with one touch or two while moving, kicking with both the right and the left foot, concentrating on vision and the position of their feet, considering both the direction the ball is coming from as well as where they are going to pass it.
As a next step I recommend 8 vs 8 matches, with possession of the ball restricted to two touches in a limited space.
Besides, **skills must be improved towards maximum accuracy at a fast pace.** From this point of view, the exercises must be carried out at different distances (in length and width, and diagonally): at 1, 3, 5-10 yards.

A More Offensive Soccer

A **more offensive soccer** can be obtained through quick passes. Brazil plays an offensive kind of soccer. The players touch the ball several times and they do not lose possession: inevitably, this results in a great deal of ball dribbling that generates an extremely offensive soccer.
There is another way to make offensive soccer, which enables the players to play more in the opponents' half of the field. This is accomplished through some forced off-side applied by the defense or with a ball played on the opposing defense and stolen to develop the action. An example of offensive soccer is the goalkeeper's return of the ball. That is, offensive soccer can be initiated by the goalkeeper sending the ball to the opposing half of the field and then play develops from there.
Two important aspects of offensive soccer are that 1) the action must be kept far from one's own goal, so risks are minimized; 2) the players should play in 30 yard sections, thus saving energy.

Exercises

The exercise shown in diagram 29 improves "geometric" passing and is useful for learning the principles of shaking off one's marker:

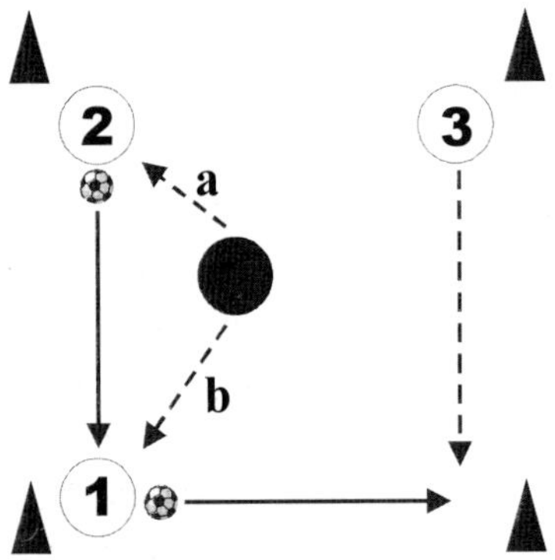

- *10x10 / 5x5 yard square*
- *3 on 1*
- *1 or 2 touches*

Diagram 29 - The ball must be passed to the corner which has been left free.

A very useful exercise to speed up movement is shown in diagram 30: player H runs to the ball sent by the coach, carries out a "stop and go" with the ball, dribbles it to the end of the field and then crosses with the left foot.
"Details" to work on: bending of the supporting leg, direction of the feet and the body.

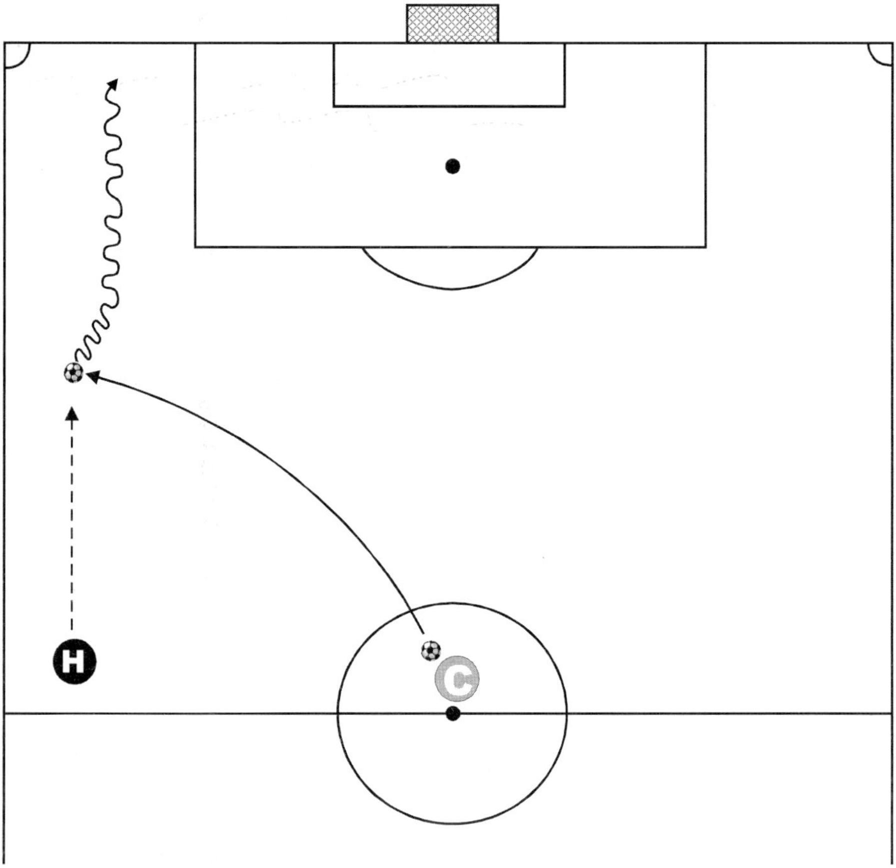

Diagram 30 - Playing the ball at full speed.

Those exercises aimed at improving technical skills (contact with the ball and kick, position of the supporting leg, position of the body, etc.) must be carried out using two, three or four players. When I observe particular weaknesses in a player, I work with the player, addressing every detail.
Every coaching activity performed by a player in total awareness yields good results: this is true also with high performance players.
As for team exercises with technical-tactical objectives, at first I usually ask the concerned section (the defense, the midfield, the attack) to carry them out; then I ask the group, that is all those players involved in the development of the action (even if they do not belong to the same section); finally, the whole team carries them out.

How to Find Space in Pressure Situations Involving "Throw-ins"

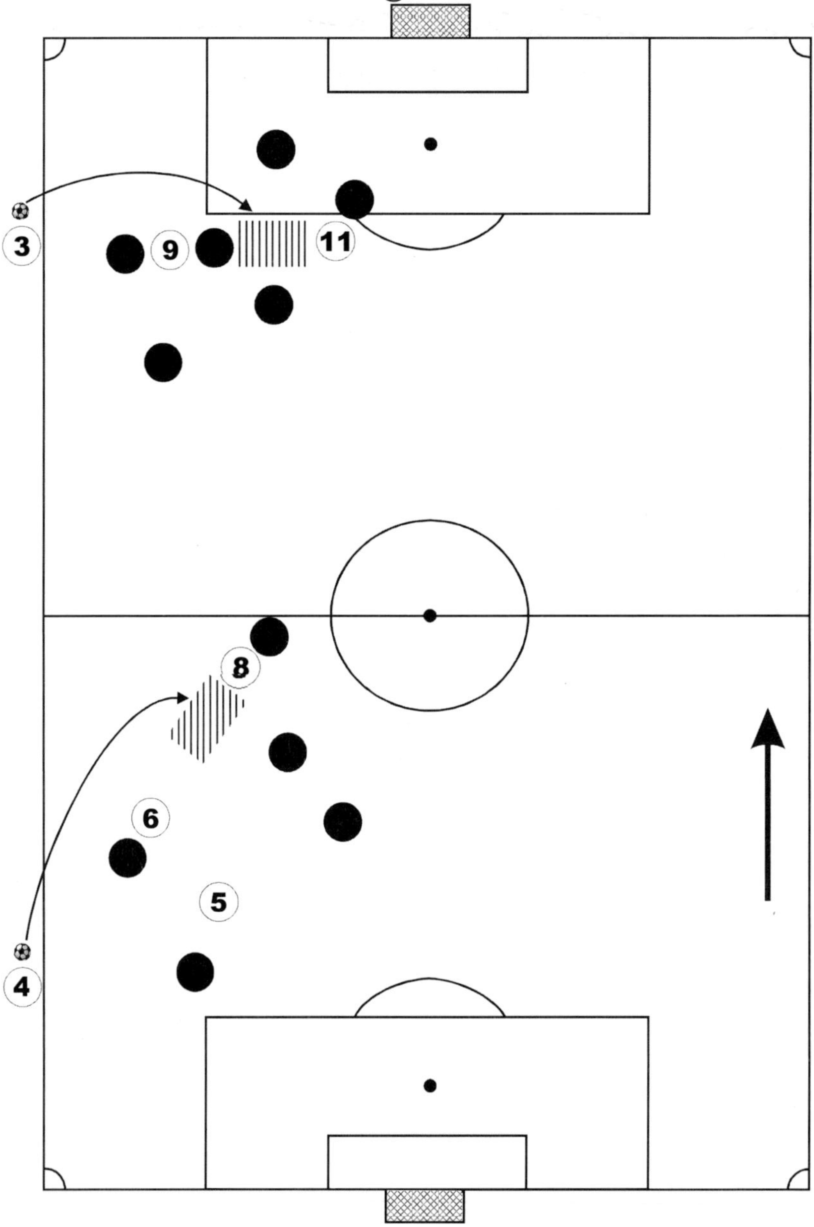

Diagram 31 - Try to find an empty space where the ball can be received.

Chapter 3

Pre-season Conditioning and Annual Workplan for a High Performance Team

- Foreword
- Pre-season conditioning
- The "Cometti" exercises
- Fitness with regard to the annual activity
- Official matches as a coaching instrument
- Nervous tension
- Annual workplan
- Reading my soccer

Foreword

Before addressing this subject I would like to make some general comments.
I have always coached high level and high performance teams (Cagliari can also be considered as such with regard to the pre-established objectives) involved ten months a year in championship, European cup and official tournament matches.
In the last years, the number of matches has increased. This has reduced the players' holidays and rest, and the summer period has been devoted to pre-season training.
The economic interests in soccer that bring loads of money to the clubs through mass-media, including television and sponsorship, has resulted in the reduction in the amount of time available for pre-season conditioning in order to give way to friendly matches and tournaments.
In theory, the ideal pre-season conditioning should be based on initial attention to general endurance, and then attention to reaching a dynamic, explosive phase of play inserted in the weekly activity and in the specific period before a match, but, as a result of the previously mentioned economic pressure, such training is fading now. A player's summer holidays are not as long as they used to be; even if a player's contract provides for four weeks' holiday, some players do not even have three, due to possible cup finals or national team matches.
This is why, in my pre-season conditioning, I start with players who still have not fully recovered, but who get fit after a few days, even if, in time, they have a psycho-physical drop-off.

Pre-season Conditioning

I have always been at ease with the "three units of work" shown in table 2, updated according to related scientific discoveries and advice given by physical conditioning trainers and researchers.

Pre-season Conditioning		
1st UNIT	**2nd UNIT**	**3rd UNIT**
❑ General endurance ❑ General strength	❑ Specific strength ❑ Aerobic power ❑ Elastic muscular endurance	❑ Specific endurance ❑ Explosiveness ❑ Activity with intervals ❑ The "Cometti" exercises

Table 2

- The first training unit starts with five days focused on endurance and general strength: runs, muscular endurance with both specific and technical graded exercises. After this first unit it is useful to play a tournament or a match in order to provide for specific activity.

- After one day's recovery (during which massages and blood tests are carried out) a second training unit starts, based on strength conditioning (of a bit more specific kind) and aerobic power conditioning related to elastic muscular endurance, using exercises carried out with light weights and technical-tactical drills. After this period, a friendly match is played for 45 to 60 minutes.

- The third training unit is made up of more specific endurance conditioning and sprint training, carried out at intervals on distances ranging from 110 to 55 and 30 yards. In this phase I apply a method that draws on the latest discoveries of a French researcher (Cometti) and is made up of mixed exercises lasting 10 to 15 seconds: sprints, take-offs, shots (movements more closely connected with soccer activity).

Such exercises in this period take the players to a condition closer to the performance standard.

Then, condition training continues with complex general activities during the coaching sessions in between matches.
We should not forget that in this pre-season training period two matches a week are usually played: therefore, adequate attention should be given to building the players' optimum physical condition while giving them adequate recovery time.
Every player's recovery time should be carefully checked: in fact, some players might "collapse" after the first friendly matches because of inadequate recovery time. For this purpose, I chart each individual player's recovery times, so that if a player plays a whole match (90 minutes), in the next match he will be given adequate recovery time. Afterwards, the player will work on the following kind of exercises. They are inserted in the period of friendly matches, but I also use them in between matches, even if in a less concentrated form.

The "Cometti" Exercises

Cometti has conceived a series of exercises made up of jumps, runs, sprints, take-offs and shots.
I have had good results with these exercises. The players carry them out with enthusiasm and interest as they are not monotonous and involve everything: sprinting, shooting, jumping, coordination (see diagram 32).

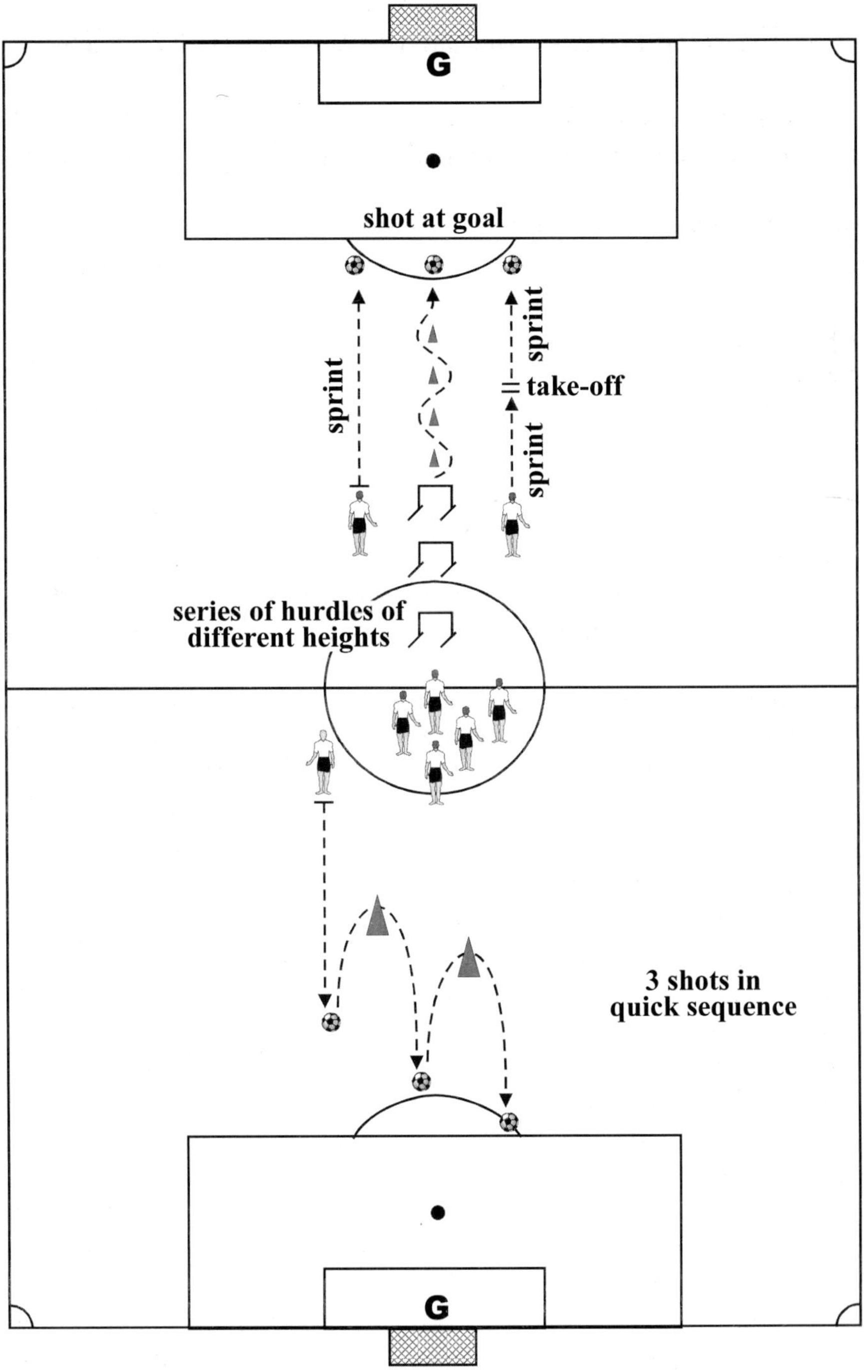

Diagram 32 - Cometti exercise.

Fitness with regard to the annual activity

My condition training takes the players to 90% of their optimum fitness level as early as the first phase of the official matches, as shown in Graph 1.

Graph 1 - Percentage of fitness related to annual activity.

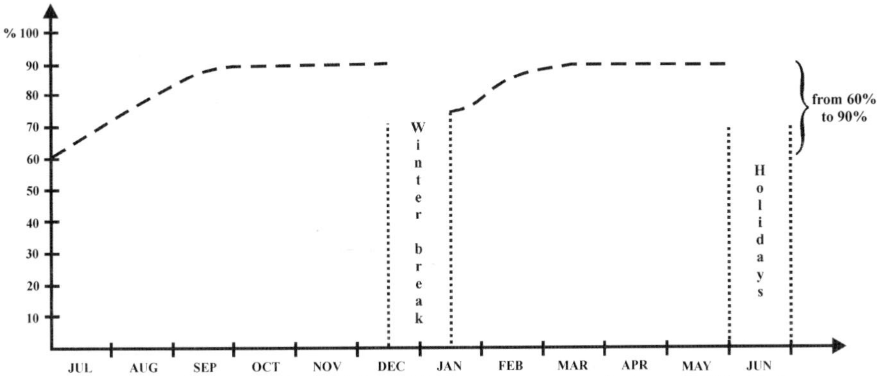

This graph is referred to the 1997/1998 soccer season of Bayern Munich.

This standard of fitness is maintained because during the monthly cycle I reuse the exercises and stimulate energy, functional aspects, condition training, that is 1-minute, 50-, 40- and 30-second repetitions.
I have learned a lot from physical conditioning trainers, even if they probably lack the **direct experience derived from "match play"**: but if a coach has also been a player, then he can understand the way a player feels on various days of the week, and so he can modify certain situations.
When the time comes for a player to play the championship match, then the cup match, then possibly the national team match, there can be different responses: some players can easily recover, some cannot.
Therefore, in a period of concentrated activity such reapplication of previously used exercises must take place at monthly intervals or during the break prior to the national team's matches. The subject of condition training is broad and may be controversial. It is both theoretical and practical, as well. In theory, in order to have adequate recovery time and good performance results, condition training should be carried out to the maximum as much as possible.
Some coaches, instead, try to get maximum effort from their teams, but, as a result, the players sometimes later become exhausted and ineffectual.

Soccer is not cyclical: it is not a 200-yard run in which, after a 30-minute recovery and the revival of energy, more energy can be burnt up. No one has ever established how much energy is burnt up during a soccer match. In the coaching session the day after the match, the players should not be pushed too hard. After 90 minutes of play, we cannot demand the same level of performance as before, or after three months the team will slip towards the bottom of the league. Some teams tend to start at a very high performance level, but then their performance drops: the players are said to be not fit, but the truth is that they exceeded their limits. They have been subjected to extra work with excessive loads which have produced no positive coaching effect.

I try to find a balance: in fact, my players always run for ten months, not like the wind, but constantly maintaining an acceptable level of conditioning.

When there has been proper conditioning, specific fitness is there at every match, just like performance.

Official Matches as a Coaching Instrument

Official matches can be considered as a coaching instrument, functioning to obtain better fitness. Therefore condition training includes official matches, which are considered as "training sequences", helping to reach optimum fitness as soon as possible.

Nervous Tension

This is another element characterizing high performance soccer. Mario Cipolla, a physician and former "Serie A" player, stimulated my reflection on this subject when he said to me: "There is so much talk about recovery, but no one has ever considered the nervous aspect, the tension before the match". No one has ever considered a player's emotions, anxiety, energy vacuum, one and a half hours before the match.

People and supporters say: "These players are being paid millions yet they do not get emotionally involved". But I have seen responsible professionals like Cabrini, Platini and many others still exhausted even three or four days after the match. Such nervous tension cannot be quantified. Only one's own experience as a coach can help. Personally, I do not require my players to carry out psycho-kinetic or reflex-based exercises when I see them tired and lethargic.

Weekly coaching is carried out two days before the match too, but the exercises are less concentrated in order not to stress the players while at the same time keeping up their physical conditioning and make their muscles work in a relaxed and effortless way.

Annual Workplan

The annual workplan must first consider the deadlines and the objectives to be accomplished. For instance, it must consider all national and European cup matches to be played during the early months of the first round of the national championship.

Besides, international soccer is changing. The Champions League could change its name and become a big European tournament. The other Cups could change too[7].

For example, Bayern Munich's annual workplan (referred to the 1997/1998 soccer season, as shown in table 3) had to be prepared considering the German championship's winter break.

Starting with the 1997/1998 season, I tried to reduce the overall period of rest to one month only, in order to take into consideration the playing schedules of other countries where there is not such a break.

---

[7] An agreement was reached between UEFA and national leagues on 23 October 1998: starting from the 1999/2000 soccer season, the European teams with the necessary requirements will be entitled to play in either of two competitions, the Champions League and the UEFA Cup (which will absorb the Cup Winners' Cup).

Bayern Munich's annual workplan:

1997/1998 soccer season
Bayern Munich's annual workplan

June 97	July 97	August 97	September 97
Holiday	friendly matches: 11-15 official matches: ▲	friendly matches: ✻ official matches: 6 ▲ + 2 LIGA	friendly matches: ✻ official matches: 4 ▲ + 2 UEFA
	% physical conditioning: 70% / % technical-tactical coaching: 30%	% physical conditioning: 50% / % technical-tactical coaching: 50%	% physical conditioning: 30% / % technical-tactical coaching: 70%

October 97	November 97	December 97	January 98
friendly matches: ✻ official matches: ■	friendly matches: ✻ official matches: ■	friendly matches: / official matches: ▲ Break	friendly matches: many official matches: / Break
% physical conditioning: 30% ⧄ / % technical-tactical coaching: 70%	% physical conditioning: 30% ⧄ / % technical-tactical coaching: 70%	% physical conditioning: 30% / % technical-tactical coaching: 70%	% physical conditioning: ●–● / % technical-tactical coaching: ●–●

February 98	March 98	April 98	May 98
friendly matches: / official matches: ■	friendly matches: ✻ official matches: ■	friendly matches: ✻ official matches: □	friendly matches: ✻ official matches: ◪
% physical conditioning: 50% / % technical-tactical coaching: 50%	% physical conditioning: 30% / % technical-tactical coaching: 70%	% physical conditioning: 30% / % technical-tactical coaching: 70%	% physical conditioning: 30% / % technical-tactical coaching: 70%

Table 3

Symbols in Bayern Munich's annual workplan:

- * Only for those not participating in official matches
- ▲ National championship calendar
- ■ National championship calendar + UEFA + Germany's Cup
- ●–● Basic conditioning resumption
- □ 4 National championship + 1 UEFA + 1 Germany's Cup matches
- ◪ 2 National championship matches + Germany's Cup final
- ⊠ Recalls of strength and lactacid power

Reading my soccer

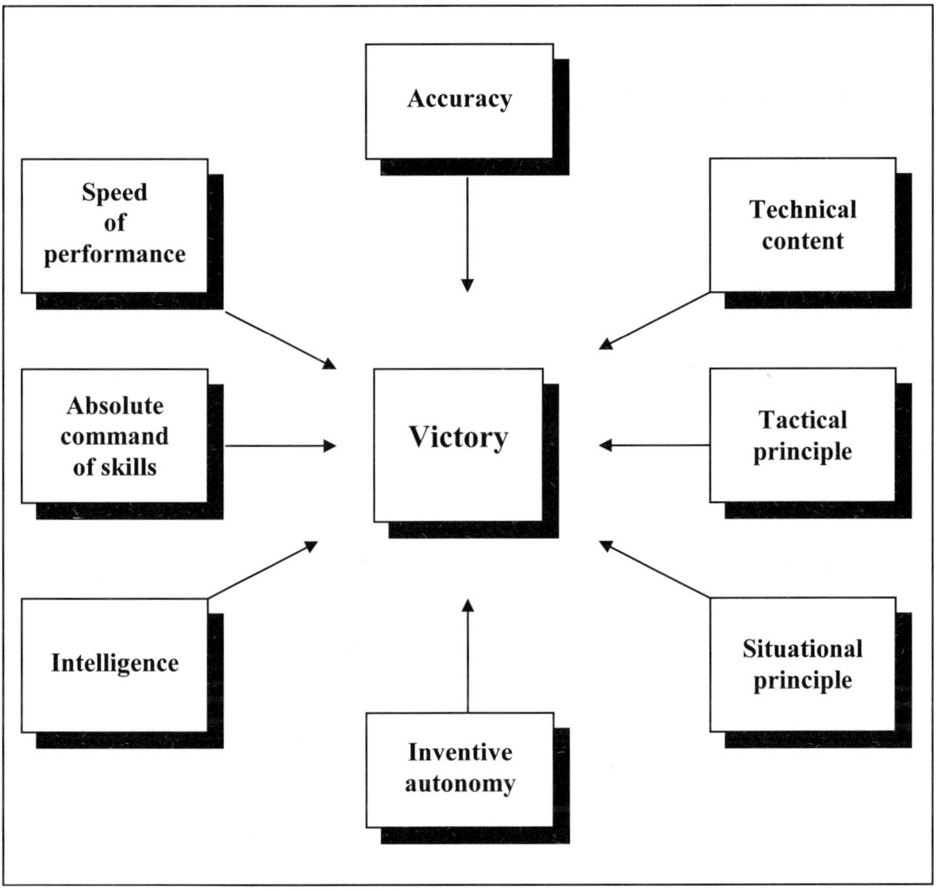

Scheme 1

Final conclusion

By G. Trapattoni

At a U.E.F.A. convention in Barcelona (February 23-27, 1998), technical manager Andy Roxburgh discussed "the Philosophy of the Coach", using the material shown on the following pages (photos 1 and 2).
The objective was to see if, in the third millennium, a universal approach to "*soccer*" could be found by comparing the opinions of a U.E.F.A. technical manager, a high performance soccer coach and a youth soccer coach. Thus, starting from the human aspect (clockwise) the comparison has given the following results.

The coach must be compassionate in his relationships with his players, conveying understanding and positive feelings that influence the player as an individual and as a thinking, autonomous and inventive being. The coach must take risks, make mistakes, admit and correct them: this is part of human nature too.

A coach is inventive when he understands and sees the opportunities to develop all the abilities of his players: he can see their improvement, potential and effectiveness. The players can improve also when they are over 30, developing some characteristics that they probably did not know or practice before.

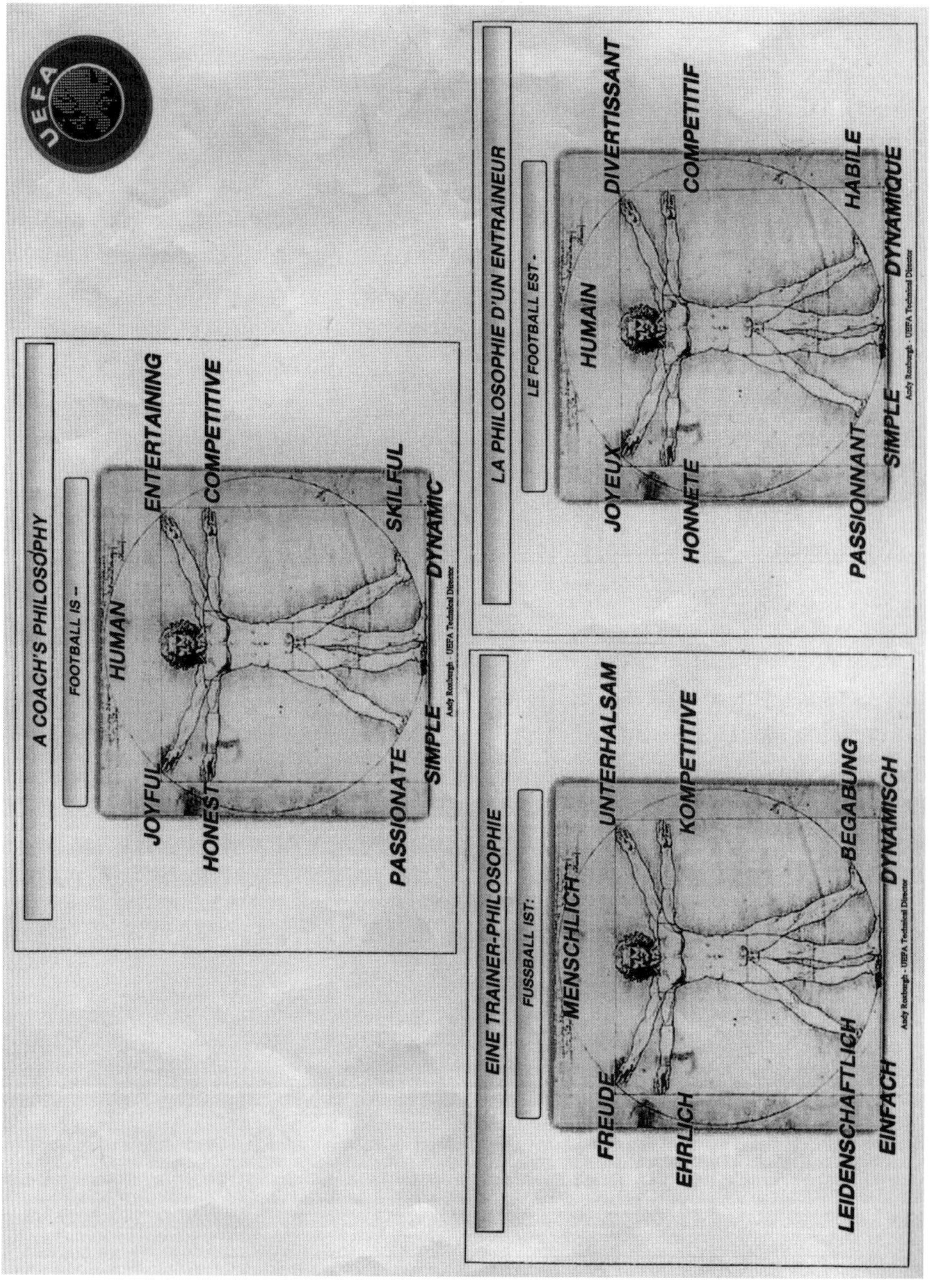
UEFA
A COACH'S PHILOSOPHY
FOOTBALL IS -
HUMAN
ENTERTAINING
COMPETITIVE
SKILFUL
DYNAMIC
SIMPLE
PASSIONATE
HONEST
JOYFUL
Andy Roxburgh - UEFA Technical Director
LA PHILOSOPHIE D'UN ENTRAINEUR
LE FOOTBALL EST -
HUMAIN
DIVERTISSANT
COMPETITIF
HABILE
DYNAMIQUE
SIMPLE
PASSIONNANT
HONNETE
JOYEUX
Andy Roxburgh - UEFA Technical Director
EINE TRAINER-PHILOSOPHIE
FUSSBALL IST:
MENSCHLICH
UNTERHALSAM
KOMPETITIVE
BEGABUNG
DYNAMISCH
EINFACH
LEIDENSCHAFTLICH
EHRLICH
FREUDE
Andy Roxburgh - UEFA Technical Director

Photo 1

A COACH'S PHILOSOPHY

Football is -

1. **HUMAN**
   - art - not science
   - players - not robots
   - risks/mistakes
2. **ENTERTAINING**
   - creative
   - dramatic
   - spectacular
3. **COMPETITIVE**
   - physical challenges
   - mental toughness
   - a winning mentality
4. **SKILFUL**
   - **Technical competence**
   - **tactical efficiency**
   - **team cohesion**
5. **DYNAMIC**
   - athletic prowess
   - lively team movement
   - ball speed
6. **SIMPLE**
   - clear rules
   - uncomplicated tactics
   - basic language
7. **PASSIONATE**
   - intense enthusiasm
   - spirit of adventure
   - love of the game
8. **HONEST**
   - sporting behaviour
   - anticorruption
   - commitment
9. **JOYFUL**
   - fun
   - pride
   - jubilation

Photo 2

The Philosophy of a Coach

Soccer is:

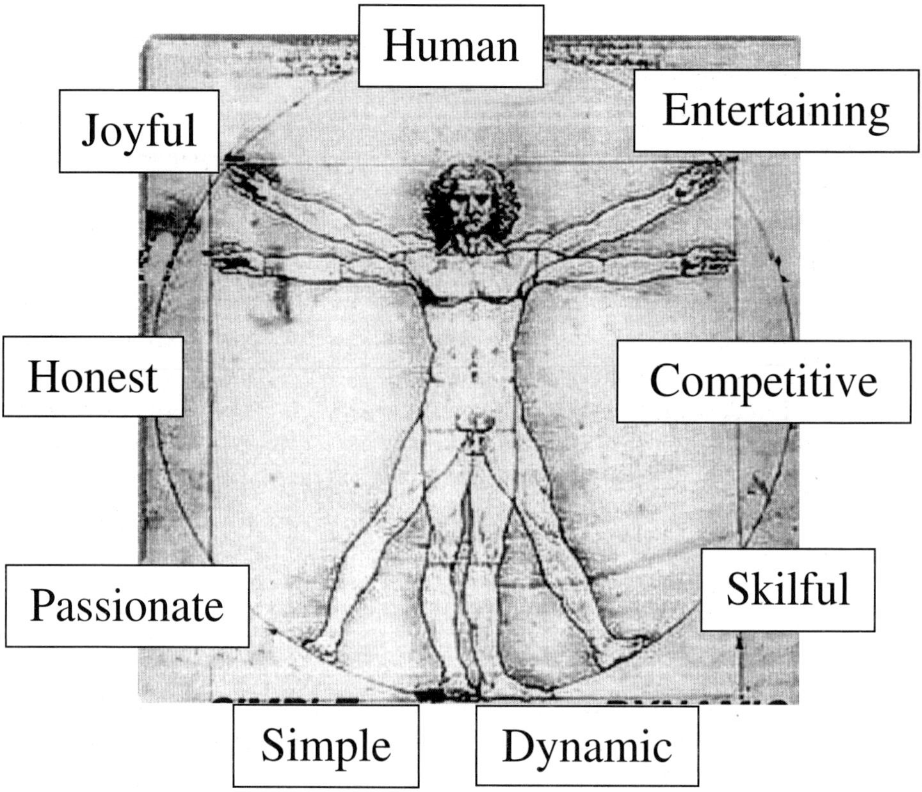

Photo 3

First of all, a coach must remain calm and focused: that is, he must understand his players and team when they face critical moments. When concentration and positive tension are needed he can stave off pressure, and place the situation in perspective when the players have done their best but the result has been negative. He understands when a player needs to be helped and reassured, to be made not to feel guilty for mistakes, as this would be very dangerous from the psychological point of view.

Competitiveness is something that one learns at school and that, partly, can be cultivated and acquired: to be successful it is necessary to be competitive and have a winning mentality. Being competitive means measuring one's strength against the opposition, never being absolutely certain of being the best. It means having a good psychological balance which results in a steady drive to continuous improvement.

A good coach immediately understands the real strength of his team and combines the qualities and abilities of his players: he can tell who has more strength, intelligence, inventiveness, creativity and who is more skilled. He optimizes the individual values of his players, positioning them in the field so as to have a maximum performance "structure".

Dynamic play, speed of the ball, team movement: it is important to continuously practice the speed of the ball in passing. The exercises have a deeper meaning when they involve movement: not only passes to empty spaces for the teammate but also timely passes towards his run. During the exercises it is very easy to notice who has developed - or is endowed with - this ability: timely and quick passes to the teammates' feet in different parts of the field. At first, I get my players used to passing the ball to their teammates while counting. That is, when they control and pass, I count "*1, 2, 3*" and the player must have already passed the ball in a precise way towards his teammate's run. Then, when the player receives the ball he must already be in a position to make the pass in the best possible way, be it a low, precision or long pass. A slow player must receive the ball at a non-excessive speed, while a quick one at a greater speed. Only a few exercises are needed to immediately understand, both in triangulations with a third moving player and in the 30/40-yard deep pass to a running teammate, that the pass must be accurate - to the feet - and not far ahead or behind, or the sweeper or a covering opponent can stop the action. Perfection is needed and the player must be carefully coached on passes.
Today, physical conditioning is certainly more important than before: the teams win possession of the ball and counterattack so frequently all through the match and this requires the players to be fit and able to constantly perform at a high level.

A coach must coach "simply" and set clear rules when he builds the team. The rules must be valid for players, coaching assistants and trainers. This simplicity can be expressed by proposing strategy, patterns and tactics based on the following principles:

- never dribble excessively;

- pass the ball as quickly as possible in depth;
- control the pace of play;
- limit risks;
- cover behind the ball;
- use tactical communication to help the teammate with the ball;
- be aware of the team's weak and strong points.

Tactics should focus on pressure to win the ball and then to quickly develop the offensive action.

A coach's passion, enthusiasm and love for soccer are vital and instrumental in determining his willingness to search for new solutions, start new initiatives, vary and differentiate the exercises that give pleasure and satisfaction to the players and the team. In this way coaching never becomes extremely repetitive. Of course, repetitions are important for learning something specific, but if they are always carried out in the same way, the players' enthusiasm can be dampened and so, in time, they can lose effectiveness.
Curiosity and a search for novelty are not to be ignored, and this applies both to players and coaches.

A sound education is based on honesty, sportsmanlike behavior and not letting others condition you. Even if sometimes an excess of competitive spirit and the determination to win might make you forget for a while the rules of sportsmanlike education, they are what you finally return to when your education is based on ethical and moral principles.

A coach must always listen to and reassure his players, be amusing and in a good mood. When he is in a bad mood, possibly due to negative results, it is important for him not to show it to the team or he could transfer it to them, with alienating results: "*come on boys, cheer up, the next time we'll have better luck...*".
Being in a good mood, reassuring and honest has always come naturally and spontaneously to me. When I think back to Juventus, Inter Milan or Bayern Munich, where I had experiences that in Italy seemed a bit heated and not really natural..., I remember how I used to present myself afterwards to my players in a joyful, honest and warm way, with the ability to change those moods which can be extremely harmful in certain moments.

We have come back to the starting point: the human aspect. My being human, conveying feelings and vibrations from my 60 years of age and 25 years of experience, is what mostly gratifies and satisfies me. Ferri, Bergomi, Cabrini, Platini, Zickler, Strunz, Fink and many others have personally confirmed this to me.
This is to stress that if a coach is fair, consistent, spontaneous and honest, the players understand him and the team can give him what he asks of them... and all together they can obtain the maximum.

It is important, both in victories and in losses, that the coach show honesty, serenity and psychological balance, both personally as well as between himself and the teammembers. Honesty, serenity and psychological balance require open and unequivocal communication with the entire environment: managers, supporters, colleagues and mass-media. Honesty, serenity and psychological balance are vital in a much too often tense and exaggerated environment which sometimes does not respect you.
Common sense is a part of your role, your person, your being human, and a part of those moral values you have inside and which you want to convey at the threshold of the third millennium, while coaching soccer.

Finally, I think that many considerations of this philosophy apply to youth soccer too, especially those tending to help the introduction, development and improvement of the young players' technical-tactical and physical aspects, trying to structure the player's education to social and moral values, his character and his personality.

A Coach's Philosophy

Soccer is:

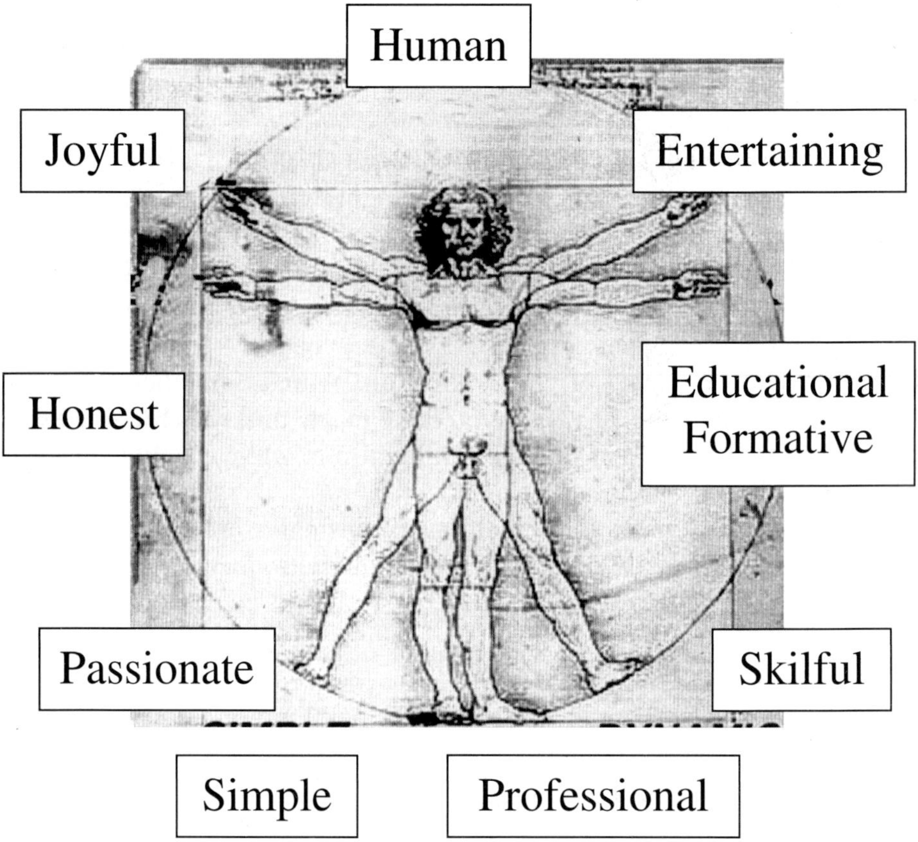

Photo 4

"How shall we finish this book, Sir?"
"Let's finish it by saying that in soccer, at any level, the movement of the legs is always determined by the brain and the heart".